VOICES FROM THE SHOPFLOOR: DRAMAS OF THE EMPLOYMENT RELATIONSHIP

For Hilary and Steve, who daily break down the binarism, and to whom I thank for a polycentric upbringing.

Voices from the Shopfloor: Dramas of the Employment Relationship

ANNE-MARIE GREENE
Lecturer in Industrial Relations, University of Warwick

Routledge
Taylor & Francis Group
LONDON AND NEW YORK

First published 2001 by Ashgate Publishing

2 Park Square, Milton Park, Abingdon, Oxon OX14 4RN
605 Third Avenue, New York, NY 10017

Routledge is an imprint of the Taylor & Francis Group, an informa business

First issued in paperback 2021

A Library of Congress record exists under LC control number: 2001022162

ISBN 13: 978-1-138-72065-7 (hbk)
ISBN 13: 978-0-367-24955-7 (pbk)

Contents

List of Plates

Acknowledgements

My greatest debt is to all those managing, representing and working at LockCo, KeyCo and the Lockunion, without whom this book would never have been written. In particular, I would like to thank Margaret Grieco for endless encouragement and helping mould the research thesis and move it forward in new directions. I would also like to thank John Black and Peter Ackers for their support, friendship and mutual industrial relations interests. I owe a huge debt of gratitude to Peter Gillam, who has offered constant emotional support throughout the trials and tribulations of both the research and the writing of this volume. I acknowledge the guidance and collegial friendship offered by the members of the Odyssey Group, Gill Kirton and the help of those involved in the production of this book series especially Pat FitzGerald and, at Ashgate, Val Rose and Anne Keirby. The photograph on page 64 has been reproduced with kind permission of the photographer Nick Hedges. Finally, I would like to thank Mike Terry, Ed Heery and Alan McKinlay for their helpful comments.

Prologue

The aim of this volume is to demonstrate the utility of ethnographic research methods to industrial relations in the developing world. The volume makes use of an ethnographic account of an occupational community based around the lock manufacturing industry in England, plus a number of ethnographically-informed industrial relations accounts from the developing world. This is in order to illustrate the vitality and richness of the ethnographic method, connecting such accounts to emergent themes, which have relevance for industrial relations in the developing world and attempting to break down the existing binarism which rigidly separates developed and developing world contexts.

This Prologue illustrates the kind of ethnographic material that informs this volume. We firstly present some examples from the lock industry ethnographies, exploring the experience of work on the assembly line in a lock factory from both the perspective of an ethnographic observer and then from the perspective of two of the assembly line workers themselves. Secondly we present a developing world example, offering citations from Ramaswamy's (1994) study of a rayon spinning factory in Delhi, India; once again from both the perspective of Ramaswamy himself as an ethnographic observer and then from the perspective of a factory worker.

The Ethnographic Researchers' View at the Lock Company

> Conditions are hard at the factory. Walking around, the noise of machinery is deafening. The most prominent image of assembly work is its fast pace. The effects of this are demonstrated by watching the women at their benches, as they rock their torsos as they work, getting into the rhythm necessary to keep the piece rate up to speed. Their hands move like lightening, picking up a component, adding it into the machine and pressing levers in a fluid motion lasting only seconds. If you talk to the women minutes after they have been working, they continue to rock in the rhythm of the line. People are machining on hand presses, sparks and splinters flying everywhere, while others are hand filing locks and keys. It is mostly the women you see on the shopfloor, many of the men are tucked away in the tool rooms, or the warehouse. Foremen, distinguishable by their red-collared blue coats, instead of overalls, walk around

the shopfloor overseeing, stopping now and then to talk to the women or to consult their clipboards. These are the lock workers.

Two Lock Assembly Workers' Views

With the miller, you put a component in, you lock your tool, you start a handle and it goes through and cuts that cut, then you have to wait for it to come back. Usually you've got your next one ready, sometimes they're pretty quick, and that might be waiting for you so the quicker you pick the next component up and get it in … the better it is … I mean I went on like a Well's press, and it ain't the original foot pedal what they used to use, and you've got to sort of sit, so you can see inside as the guard opens, the chairs are too high or too low, and me being pretty tall, you know, … you've got to sit on the edge of your seat, … you were sort of having to really press down before anything would happen, and then as the day wore on, my back, every time I touched the treadle, I could feel it jarring my back.

… when I joined here when I was fifteen, I thought I'd got the world, but I wanted to look after children, and … I thought, 'When I'm sixteen, I'll leave and do what I want to do', but I got into a crowd, and they was near enough my age, eighteen upwards, and they made me feel that welcome, and you sit in a group sort of thing, and we had that many laughs and that much fun, it weren't like coming to work, it was a pleasure, you know … I love coming to work, I love it here, I do, ask anyone, they'll say I'm bleeding mental, gotta be, ain't you cock, to get on.

The Ethnographic Researcher's View at the Indian Rayon Spinning Factory

Important differences in technology and the structure of work in the three segments of the factory – pulp, fibre and yarn – have always influenced the thinking of both labour and management. The pulp plant is by far the most highly automated of the three. Manual work here is largely confined to the start of the process, where crane operators load logs onto chippers, and at the end of the line where unskilled labourers stack the pulp boards. In between lies typical process technology which makes few demands on workers during normal times. They have little work, except to watch instrument panels and note down readings. The pace of work is distinctly easy. For both workers and management, in sum, pulp represented a better place (Ramaswamy, 1994, p. 27).

The Factory Workers' View at the Rayon Spinning Factory

> The pulp operator who was heading for the night shift complained about the boredom of his routine: 'I can sit down, relax and take some rest, but can't doze. My luck is so rotten that the process which works perfectly when I am around would develop a snag if I take a wink. The management won't go beyond a memo, but how would I face 2000 workers? Everyone would comment that in spite of 25 years in the pulp plant, I allowed an entire batch to be ruined. I take a book with me to keep me awake' (pulp operator quoted in Ramaswamy, 1994, p. 136).

The above text illustrates the way in which the ethnographic observer's view is complemented and challenged by the voiced accounts of the people researched, in both developed and developing contexts. These short accounts give a glimpse of some of the themes to emerge within the volume, notably the need to see industrial relations as a complex web of social interactions, where, for example harsh work conditions are alleviated by social contact, or where social group or occupational community pressure plays a part in ensuring quality control and work commitment.

This volume is about the relationships, interactions, memories and histories that make up industrial relations, brought alive on the page through the discourse of those involved. It is through ethnography that such stories are possible.

Chapter One

Focusing on the Interior of Social Action: the Contribution of Ethnographic Approaches to Industrial Relations

The quantitative approach dominates the industrial relations field. As a consequence, we contend that the industrial relations literature for developing countries is severely underdeveloped as a consequence of the rigid hold of quantitative industrial relations paradigms over the discipline. In addition, many developing countries do not have the statistical bases or the resources to build the statistical bases, which would generate industrial relations literature within the prevailing paradigm. Ethnography is an appropriate methodology for exploring industrial relations. This volume thus opens the gate to industrial relations voices from the developing world by establishing the prestige and current contribution of ethnographic methods within this policy and academic domain. It makes links between the analysis presented and its methodology with a model for industrial relations research within the developing world context.

Before specifically looking at industrial relations research in the developing world, some background discussion is necessary. Both the quantitative, macro-level survey and the micro-level case study have a long history within industrial relations inquiry in Britain, North America and Australia. However, two more recent areas of debate in the field have relevance for the methodology proposed within this volume. The first involves concerns raised by researchers about the growing predominance of the quantitative survey as an industrial relations methodology while the second deals with calls for voiced accounts, where the voices of those involved in the research: their thoughts, comments, observations and actions can be directly seen and heard in the text.

Marginson (1998) summarises the concerns raised by a number of researchers about the demise of the tradition of case-study research and the spread of research based on analysis of survey data sets (Brown and Wright, 1994; Kelly, 1994; McCarthy, 1994). In contrast to fears that the survey method is being rejected, Whitfield and Strauss (1998) trace the increasing use of quantitative methods in industrial relations research in Britain and North America. A quick glance through latest editions of industrial relations journals will attest to the predominance of quantitative research material. Indeed Strauss and Whitfield state that the editorial system of those journals deemed to be of the highest quality, 'encourages safe, narrow articles that can pass the scrutiny of often hostile reviewers. Most journals today seem to prefer highly empirical studies, highly buttressed with statistics' (1998, p. 18). In addition, the accessibility of survey data sets such as the Workplace Employee Relations Survey (Cully et al., 1999) in Britain and the technology capable of analysing it, has meant that quantitative surveys are more popular in that they have the capability to generate high productivity for academics in terms of publication (Kelly, 1994). We need to begin now however, to question whether this is really generating quality of inquiry and account.

The emergence of the survey as the predominant paradigm is of concern because it is felt that the survey method is limited in uncovering processes behind structures and practices (Edwards, 1995) and emphasises explanations focused on structures and environments rather than processes and actions (Kelly, 1994). Morris and Wood (1992) also identify that surveys tend to emphasise continuity rather than change. While surveys are often held up as providing fruitful starting points for further case studies (Morris and Wood, 1992), the opposite is also true, that more qualitative approaches can provide challenges to and support for generalised survey findings. Terry and Edwards (1988), make a specific call for more industrial relations studies at the level of individual plant or company, to complement the broader historical accounts, which emphasise patterns across whole industries.

Within the developing world context specifically, the factors presented as being particular strengths of the quantitative survey can present clear difficulties. Marginson (1998, p. 365) outlines two main strengths of the most recent quantitative British industrial relations surveys in comparison to those earlier surveys, which he feels are more open to criticism:

> the ability of such surveys to provide an account of structures and practices that is representative of workplaces or large enterprises, across the economy ... flows from the use of proper statistical sampling procedures and rigorous fieldwork methods. Provided that a high level of response is elicited, the findings from the sample survey can be generalised ... The principal methodological disadvantage confronting the earlier, pre-1980, workplace surveys lay in the unavailability of a suitable comprehensive listing of the population of workplaces across the economy ... from which an economy-wide representative sample could have been drawn.

If generalisability underpins the contribution of surveys within industrial relations, then one must seriously consider whether such a methodology is appropriate for the developing world context. In the development field, researchers and academics confess the difficulty that is confronted in conducting large scale survey research in many countries in the developing world where such comprehensive population lists are not available, nor the statistical databases to develop such resources (Ravi Kanbur, personal communication).

The second area of new debate, involves calls for voiced accounts within industrial relations in order to expand the issues researched beyond simply bargaining within organisations. Seeing industrial relations as about social interactions and relational processes directs one to methods that have a greater participatory dimension such as ethnography.

An Ethnographic Approach: Voicing the Accounts

A gap in the industrials relations field is only significant if an alternative offers benefits. In order to outline a possible alternative, there is a need to elucidate what we mean by ethnography and the value of it as a set of methods for industrial relations. Ethnography is not easy to circumscribe and there appears to be considerable diversity in the prescription and practice of it. Indeed in his discussion of the roots and development of ethnography, Linstead states, 'the term "ethnography" covers a diversity of positions, at the level of technique, methodology, or epistemology' (1993, p. 100). Looking at 'ethnography' in purely etymological terms, the word ethnography means the art and science of describing a group or culture, usually involving an exploration of the history of the group, the geography of location, kinship patterns, symbols, politics, economic systems, educational and socialisation systems and the degree of contact between target culture and main stream culture. However, this simplistic definition does not really capture the essence of the ethnographic approach. Essentially, ethnography is all about detail; providing rich description, sensitivity to perceptions and above all, paying attention to the voices of those people being researched. It has evolved essentially from anthropological research and so with regard to the basic elements of ethnography, in classic anthropological terms, the main technique involves participant observation. Hammersley and Atkinson characterise ethnographic participant observation as:

> The ethnographer participates overtly or covertly in people's daily lives for an extended period of time; watching what happens, listening to what is said, asking questions, collecting whatever data are available to throw light on the issue with which he or she is concerned (1983, p. 3).

However, a purist view of ethnography where it includes *only* participant observation appears to be particularly narrow and constricted. The practical contingencies of fieldwork mean that a 'full-blown', classical ethnography is often impossible. The ability to be a participant observer is limited to the extent that a lucky access situation exists or the study is in a work place that does not require particular qualifications (Czarniawska-Jeorges, 1992). In addition, this kind of participation requires a time context that is quite impractical in most cases.

Friedman and McDaniel (1998, pp. 115–16) outline four main features that offer a broader definition of ethnography, within an industrial relations arena. Firstly, direct and personal observation of people and situations. Within ethnography, a more critical and interpretative approach is preferred, which sees as its ultimate aim, an increased understanding of the social worlds researched. The main interest is in exploring more closely, the dynamics of the employment relationship and trying to investigate the social relations of work related to particular contexts, looking at how people create and legitimate their worlds. Secondly, the 'voicing' of accounts is emphasised, so that prominence is given to the words, interpretations and experiences of the people studied. This involves a concern to study: 'the frame of reference within which the actor's own definitions of the situations in which they are engaged are taken as an initial basis for the explanation of their social behaviour and relations' (Goldthorpe et al., 1968, p. 184) which emerges from older industrial sociological enquiries. One needs to investigate this process of accounting: how do people express and legitimate their social world? Ethnography is thus largely about capturing voices: one has to look for the meaning attributed to those actions by the people being researched themselves. The ethnographer relies on the spoken interpretations of those people involved and then tries to use external concepts, value systems and ideologies to help interpret them (Czarniawrska-Jeorges, 1992).

Therefore, thirdly, observations and analyses are made in the context of the people going about daily business and interacting with others. Ethnography focuses explicitly on the social context and people interacting within this context, rather than more positivistic and quantitative research techniques, in which the focus is on individuals in isolated situations and where the premise is on the need for objectivity. Industrial relations analyses within ethnographies should thus be situated firmly in their workplace contexts, focusing in on the discourses of individuals, building up 'thick description' (Geertz, 1973) by overlaying different viewpoints, observations, rhetoric and factual information derived from a variety of sources. This is a central premise: the need for the voices of the employees, managers and trade unionists to come through into the account, rather than solely from the mouth of the apparently objective researcher.

Finally, these observations from the researcher arc then shared with the reader. Thus, the researcher needs to be extremely reflexive about the research process and reflexivity represents a framework in which to regard the authenticity of an ethnographic account (Hammersley and Atkinson, 1983; Hammersley, 1992; Potter, 1996; Linstead, 1993). The most important thing is that any interpretations of the meanings attributed by the participants and any analysis of what people say and do are made explicit. Such a viewpoint attempts to overcome some of the weaknesses of many ethnographic accounts that they describe the particular social realm as 'it really is', or that it is a 'true account' (Hammersley, 1992; Rosaldo, 1989). This is particularly within the anthropological tradition, where the ethnographer's ability to describe what has been seen and heard within the framework of the social group's view of reality, is considered to be one of the primary contributions of ethnography (Fetterman, 1989). The presentation of findings from the view of the participants is however, largely an ideal and all social scientists attribute a point of view and interpretations to the people whose actions they analyse. In essence, we can only aim to present with the most practical accuracy what people think they are doing, what meanings they give to the objects and events in their lives and experience (Geertz, 1973, p. 23). This is done by allowing the voices of those researched to come through within the text, allowing the reader some space to assess whether the researchers' evaluations and explanations are appropriate.

Dramaturgical Analysis

As the title of this volume suggests, we are also concerned to present in our analysis, what we have defined as various 'dramas' of the employment relationship. Dramaturgical conceptions of social relations accept a view that there are certain accepted understandings about forms of interaction, which can be seen as involving the existence of certain roles, within certain contexts, with certain vocabularies, demanding certain behaviours, akin to the workings of a scripted play. A dramaturgical perspective on social action concerns how people (defined as social 'actors'), use impression management behaviours to create and maintain identities. Impression management (in a broad definition) is seen as part of an everyday process of socially 'constructing' reality (Gardner and Avolio, 1998), which fits with the subject matter commonly researched within ethnography. Such a view is drawn essentially from the work of Erving Goffman (1959), *The Presentation of Self in Everyday Life*, where people are seen as 'actors' engaging in 'performances', in certain 'settings' for a particular 'audience'. Use of dramatic terminology, notably, 'framing', 'scripting', 'staging' and 'performing' constitutes the phases of this dramaturgical process (Gardner and Avolio, 1998, p. 32). An emphasis is placed on the interaction between actors, so that the meaning of people's action is found in the manner in which they express themselves, within a context of that interaction with other similarly expressive people (Brissett and Edgeley, 1990). This highlights the existence of a two-way dramaturgical process, where leaders and followers jointly construct their identities and establish boundaries on appropriate behaviour and action: in terms of the dramaturgical vocabulary, the 'role' or 'part' that the leader should play. In the context of particular leaders in the workplace (whether that be union or management), the ability of leaders picking up on 'signals' emanating from the 'audience' or followers (in the employment context: employees or workers) is thus important. The idea of this two-way dramaturgical process is brought out very clearly in this volume, where contextualised worker expectations are found to influence perceptions and attitudes towards both union and management, and consequently levels of trust and commitment. The objective in using a dramaturgical perspective is not in developing new models of impression management (for a review of current research around these issues see Gardner and Avolio, 1998), but as a way of analysing the importance of leadership and management styles in influencing perceptions of commitment and trust, the acceptance or rejection of workplace restructuring and change programmes, and the mobilisation and maintenance of collective support and action.

Ethnographic Methods and the Developing World Context

In the development arena, concerns for voicing of accounts have become an important agenda item. There is a growing concern that development policy should involve more of a dialogue, rather than relying on the monologue of the 'Western expert'. As Slim and Thompson state: 'it is no longer enough for the development "expert" to summarise and interpret the views of others, the "others" must be allowed to speak for themselves' (1993, p. 2). Development agencies are making increasing efforts to canvass the views and opinions of people in the areas where they intervene as is demonstrated with the World Development Report on Poverty (www.worldbank.org/devforum/forum_poverty.html). Currently, the paradigm established within developing world industrial relations supports the rendering of only the formal account and captures only a small segment of the population. Conventional methods predominantly only capture the formal record, which would tend to exclude a large proportion of the developing world who are illiterate and who have no formal voice within the economic, political or social sphere. Those most excluded from formal policy-making thus remain voiceless. In comparison, ethnography provides a methodology that captures the informal (Thompson and Ackroyd, 1999, p. 51), which would give the illiterate a voice allowing analysis of their discourse and action.

Development theory as it has emerged in academic institutions has tended to be premised on the mechanical application of methodologies and research findings derived from the political economies of the West (Sathyamurthy, 1999). This is a significant weakness when one considers that industrial relations behaviours and institutions may have very different meanings and functions in differing cultures (Whitefield and Strauss, 1999). We need to recognise that within this rigid paradigmatic translation, there is an implicit discrediting or unwillingness to view alternative models to those of the West (Sathyamurthy, 1999). As Sathyamurthy continues, and as the later analysis of the use of qualitative methodologies within developing world industrial relations research will support, new areas of research at the macroscopic level, have been almost always carried out at the expense of the microscopic. Yet, it is at this level that we are more likely to have greater understanding of the everyday relationships between management and labour, and what consequences such understandings may have for more macro economic and industrial policies. Part of industrial relations obviously relates to social behaviour and Redding points to the requirement of access to 'indigenous frameworks of meanings' (1994, p. 344) if we are to understand organisational behaviour comparatively across countries. As Redding continues, this 'may require a radical ethnographically based challenge' to the 'bankruptcy of empirical positivism'. Such an ethnographic position holds a conviction that the 'deterministic mechanical causal model of the natural sciences is inappropriate for the enterprise of social science' (ibid., p. 347). In the field of industrial relations, this could be turned around to state that such a model is inappropriate for the 'social science of the enterprise'.

Yet currently, there exist few practical suggestions of how industrial relations research in the developing world should be carried out. In reviewing the recent 1998 book edited by Whitfield and Strauss, *Researching the World of Work: Strategies and methods in studying industrial relations*, Hawes concludes his review by noting that the book:

> is centred entirely on Australasia, North America and Britain. It includes almost no serious discussion of how qualitative and quantitative methods might need to be adapted in the Moslem, South American, Eastern, African and broader European worlds (1999, p. 539).

There is thus a need to develop new ways of thinking about industrial relations research and looking at studies that appear to offer a different approach. This is particularly as there is a significant lack of industrial relations ethnographies within the developing world context.

Existing Use of Ethnographic Methodologies in Developing World Industrial Relations

In attempting to sketch the field in terms of the use of ethnographic methodologies in industrial relations-related research in the developing world, a good starting point is to conduct bibliographical searches of the most relevant facilities. In Britain, searches were made at the British Library and at the School of Oriental and African Studies (SOAS), University of London. Such searches leave no doubt that ethnographic research has not began to hold a place with the current industrial relations paradigms in the developing world. The data sets are particularly weak in this area. For example typical Boolean keyword searches at SOAS, making connections between ethnography and labour relations or industrial relations, yielded no entries whatsoever. When the search was limited to purely ethnography and particular regions, Africa yielded 23, of which none were industrial relations-related; India yielded nine, of which only one was industrial relations-related; while a search for Asia or South East Asia yielded none at all. It is true that assertions of the apparent paucity of material in the area of industrial relations studies within an ethnographic paradigm, based on keyword searches, are somewhat misleading. Indeed, what is signalled as relevant within a Boolean keyword search is very dependent on the characteristics of the database and the keywords that are entered as relevant for that piece of material. For instance, while few entries emerged at SOAS when connecting 'ethnography' and 'Africa', there is a large collection of African anthropological work there, where ethnography is the predominant methodology. On the other hand, authors are usually asked for relevant search keywords to be assigned to their texts, and the fact that industrial relations and ethnography are linked very seldom as keywords, is of some significance in assessing the dominance of the particular research paradigm within current industrial relations research.

Certainly, the field of industrial relations itself has some standing in the developing world: searches in Africa and India found a number of related texts (although still relatively few, being 42 and 36 respectively). Searches in South East Asia again yielded few entries, with only three industrial relations-related texts found on the database with these keyword attributions. Further weaknesses within the data sets are identified when these searches are investigated more closely. Of the 42 African industrial relations texts, only 12 involved at least qualitative and case study research. For the 36 studies in India, only 11 were similarly coming close to research within a qualitative paradigm. When one looks for voicing techniques within these case studies, the data set is reduced still further, only one among the Indian studies and two among the African.

It was a similar experience when searching the undeniably larger collections on offer at the British Library. Ethnographic works in India are plentiful, indeed the anthropological village study is a well developed research method (see Bardhan, 1989) while the academic community is well established in India, with many universities having their own presses for the production of monographs and research studies. However, these village studies, while having subjects of obvious relevance to industrial relations, tend to be developed within the sphere of cultural anthropological study, and therefore without direct relevance to the world of work. Urban anthropological studies, where connections to industrial relations issues are commonly located, are more difficult to find more recently, after a period of ascendancy in the 1970s (Curtis, 1999). Overall, there is a much-reduced data set of industrial relations studies of the 'voiced' kind in both India and Africa. The overall data set available is comprised of predominantly quantitative and macro-level surveys, while case studies either make no use of voicing at all, or are purely descriptive, being voiced accounts with little or no analysis or theorising.

There are a number of interesting studies which appeared to offer the potential of valuable understanding of industrial relations situations and which would have been enriched by ethnographic methodologies and analysis. For example, Kulshereshtha's (1996) study of child labour in the Aligarh lock industry involves a fairly detailed case study, in-depth interviewing and observation approaches. However such richness of detail is not brought out in the analysis, indeed the findings are presented purely from the viewpoint of the objective researcher, with the voices of those child labourers being notably absent. These illiterate children are perhaps one of the most voiceless segments of society.

In a similar way, Bannerjee (1985, p. 4) comments in the introduction to her book on Bangladeshi women workers that:

> the drama in the situation of these workers as presented by each of the women was so moving and so rich in suggested hypotheses about this world, that one could not resist the temptation of citing individual cases.

Such promise of the vitality of account and voicing, which is suggested by these assertions, are not however lived out in the substance of the volume, in which the voices of the women and these individual cases are notably lacking, replaced instead by 'objective' analysis of the arguably less interesting survey data.

At the other end of the spectrum, Moulik and Purushotham's (1986) study of technology transfer within rural industries, and Kramsjo and Wood's (1992) study of trade union and other collective action among Bangladesh's rural poor, offers great promise of rich ethnographic accounts, making use of contextualised case studies, direct reportage and verbatim quotes. However, while these case studies are extremely interesting, in the case of the former, there is no consistent format to the accounts, where the 11 case studies vary in their use of voiced material with some being pure monologue accounts of particular individuals, while others use no voiced material at all. More importantly, in the case of both volumes, there was little direct analysis, explanation or theorising attached to the voiced accounts.

What is needed is an integrated approach, where industrial relations studies use a variety of ethnographic methods to elucidate situations, relations and experiences and use these to develop theorising about key concepts and issues. Such an attempt is made in the lock industry ethnographies referred to throughout this volume.

Focusing on the Specific Ethnography and Temporality of Locks and Keys

The empirical material referred to in this volume draws on research within the British lock industry, situated in the West Midlands and specifically around two organisations which we call LockCo and KeyCo. This meets many of the criteria, which have been established as important within industrial relations ethnography. Firstly, it has involved research over a considerable period of time. Few investigations of industrial relations that are focused on a specific enterprise have been longitudinal. This research in the West Midlands lock industry provides an account of the industrial relations climate in a manufacturing firm from the early 1980s to the late 1990s. In terms of the voices heard, managers appear out of the perceptions of workers and trade unionists: the view of management in the investigation of the employment relationship is given from a bottom-up perspective. By design, this was a view from the shopfloor, offering an interpretation of questions through an in-depth analysis of the views, opinions, attitudes, behaviour, vocabulary and rhetoric of a group of workers across the whole time period. It is the voices of the shopfloor workers and the shopfloor activists that are heard and through whose eyes, the employment relationship is viewed.

It draws primarily upon a large quantity of qualitative data amounting to around 150 in-depth interviews, numerous periods of observation, informal contact, observant participation (through key actors writing diaries) and generally 'hanging around' from four time periods at LockCo. This provides more than just a selection of snapshots, having had the opportunity to talk to workers who were part of the studies in the early 1980s and who are still employed at the research firm. This allowed a means of tapping into change and continuity in perceptions of the employment relationship over the period and how they are affected by the wider social, political, economic and ideological environment, the strategies of managers and trade union and the influence of their families and local community. Secondly, a comparison is made with another lock company KeyCo, in the 1990s context involving interviews with workers and union activists and periods of observation within the same remit. This indicated the ways in which issues of union leadership, the bargaining relationship and perceptions of trust and commitment, could be dramatically affected by significant change within the managerial structures and strategies of an organisation. The emphasis is clearly on building up a rich picture of the local context, looking at how the specific organisational context and environment have evolved together, facilitating understanding of the patterns of relationships inherent in the nature of those contexts. Through ethnographic inquiry, we begin to understand the complex and interconnected relationships between work, family and community, and the ambivalence, contradictions, as well as consistencies in views and opinions. All of this is embedded within observation of interactions in situ and combined with an understanding of historical experiences and expectations.

Some elaboration on the character of the lock companies and of the occupational community is necessary, in order to alert the reader to the importance of ethnography in understanding industrial relations in these particular workplaces. The lock industry is somewhat unique in the context of modern manufacturing in Britain. It is based in a small and defined geographical area: 90 per cent of firms and 70 per cent of the industry's employment continues to be concentrated in one relatively small town in the West Midlands. It also has a long legacy of occupational community based around the industry, both lock companies studied share very similar historical traditions, being founded in the mid-nineteenth century and still bearing the names of their founding families. As the two largest employers in the industry, they have dominated local employment since their formation and are based on a tightly knit, localised work force. Most employees still live in the industrial town, and many within walking distance of the factories, reinforcing the sense of occupational community. In many respects, the companies fit into an anatomy of paternalism (Ackers and Black, 1991; Ackers, 1998), with traditions of family firm atmosphere, community role, paternalist management style, and movement up the company hierarchy from shopfloor to managerial level. Families had legacies of employment within the companies, sons and daughters following fathers and mothers.

The industry also has a long history of moderate trade unionism. De facto closed shops exist at both firms. Matching the 'family' atmosphere of the companies, there was a large degree of social familiarity between members and full-time officials, fostered by the very low ratio of full-time officers to members (see Black et al., 1997). The industrial relations atmosphere at both plants had historically been characterised by cooperative relations between union and management within a tradition of pluralism, centred on the industrial union. The union has a history of close links with the employers, which has been a long standing tradition among the Midlands small metal trades since around the time that the union was formed (Stenner, 1989, pp. 1–13).

Both companies had demonstrated a high degree of continuity until the late 1980s with regard to the nature of work organisation and managerial responses to economic and market pressures. The situation changed during the late 1980s recession when employment in the industry fell severely due to a general downturn in worldwide sales (DTI, 1996, p. 13). Following a takeover by a UK based multinational in 1988, KeyCo experienced a complete change of management personnel (many of whom were brought from outside of the industry), the introduction of cellular organisation of work, the abolition of piecework and its replacement by cashless pay and measured day work. In addition, there was an extensive rationalisation of labour. In February 1997, the multinational brought both LockCo and KeyCo under one ownership. The old management team at LockCo was made redundant and LockCo management was placed in control of the restructuring process. Thus, at the time of the latest fieldwork in 1997–98, LockCo faced plans for similar rationalisation and dramatic restructuring of work organisation to that experienced at KeyCo and redundancies of around two hundred had been proposed. Cellular manufacturing and the abolition of piecework were being negotiated. Thus while at different stages along the process, union leaders and employees faced similar challenges and developments. Indeed KeyCo was used as an 'prototype' for LockCo and as many of the managers were shared after the takeover, much of managerial practice, as well as the change programme, were replicated at LockCo.

This brief outline of the local context is useful in that it 'sets the scene' for many of the issues that will be discussed throughout the chapters of this volume. The lock industry was a rich research context for demonstrating the utility and value of an ethnographic approach to industrial relations, allowing clear connections and interconnections to be drawn between relational processes, interaction and structures within the workplace, and relations outside of the workplace, namely family and community. Our intention is to use the ethnography of the lock companies as a way of demonstrating the utility, value and richness of the ethnographic account to industrial relations research, and in so doing elucidate its value to understanding industrial relations in the developing world. One should not think that what happens in the developed world has little relevance for greater understanding of what is happening in the developing world context and vice versa. We should be moving away from analyses, which maintain a rigid binarism between the developed and developing, traditional and modern, new and old, particularly within the globalised economy. This volume will demonstrate clearly that such binarism needs to be challenged, and will do this by constantly looking across and making comparison between the developed and the developing world. In meeting these aims, it should be noted that this volume is not a monograph. The ethnography of the lock companies is not presented wholly, or as a seamless story, such as might be expected in a conventional anthropological ethnography. The aim is to draw out some selected themes from the lock case (Greene, 1999), those which are most interesting and have greater relevance for industrial relations in the developing world, and demonstrate the utility of the ethnographic method in drawing out a richness of account.

Voice and Participation in the Processes of Industrial Relations

Currently, new technology and social policy developments have generated a demand for materials that have a stronger participatory dimension. This is particularly the case where paradigms such as the 'Third Way' raise issues about fundamental consensus building and development. The view that there is an increasing need for development policies to involve those who will be affected, in the development of those policies, is becoming widespread. Voiced accounts are very necessary and yet we have indicated how few currently exist, not only in the developed world, but even more so in the developing.

We can however find a few examples of valuable voiced industrial relations accounts. The exceptions to the dominant paradigm within industrial relations research in the developing world are quite outstanding, probably because they are so exceptional in the field. One such example is Bruce Kapferer's (1972) *Strategy and Transaction in an African Factory*. The scope of Kapferer's analysis is vast, including a six month period of in depth research at the factory site, involving interviews, observation, informal meetings, research in social surroundings such as the local beer halls, and contextualised with a full year of fieldwork in the local Bisa community where Kapferer lived and researched and supplemented by two social surveys in the local community. Kapferer was able to draw on a considerable period of time spent in the local community before beginning the research. The evaluation and theorising of descriptive voiced accounts of the labour relations of this workplace, are brought alive within the text; for example evaluations of the exchange relationship which develops between Patel the manager and the activist workers who have the resources to secure the compliance of the workgroup. While the theoretical conclusions reached by Kapferer have been the source of debate (see Burawoy, 1974), that the methodology of the study is a model of that which has been outlined in this volume as appropriate for an industrial relations study in the developing world, is beyond question. A similar methodology is undertaken by Burawoy himself in his (1974) study of a Zambian copper mine. The debate between Burawoy and Kapferer indicates the way in which the rich findings of ethnographic study can be built upon and developed and where real theorising can emerge from the voiced accounts. We will draw on Kapferer and Burawoy throughout this volume in making comparisons and drawing parallels.

Industrial relations is multi-disciplinary and given this, voiced accounts in other academic disciplines can be identified which have a lot of industrial relations significance. Such is the case with Grieco et al. (1996) *At Christmas and on Rainy Days: Transport, travel and the female traders of Accra.* Here research within the sociology of transport field, is conducted within a broad ethnographic paradigm, with the voiced accounts and the analysis of these accounts, saying a great deal about the dynamics of industrial relations of the traders in Accra. Relations between male and female traders, issues of gendered skills, the interface between work and communities, and relations within the trader hierarchies are all explored and will be referred to within the analysis of this volume.

An exception within a purely industrial relations sphere is Ramaswamy's (1994) *The Rayon Spinners: The strategic management of industrial relations.* This text, like Kapferer's, is a wonderful example of a rich industrial relations study carried out within a broad ethnographic paradigm, looking at the dynamics of industrial relations at a workplace level. Not only does the author describe himself as an industrial relations researcher, but uses, and moreover is happy to profess to using, 'methods developed by sociologists and anthropologists' (Ramaswamy, 1994, p. 21). There are remarkable similarities between the methodology of this study of one Delhi enterprise and that of the West Midlands lock companies. Exactly parallel to that at LockCo, Ramaswamy conducted his fieldwork over a 15 year period, returning to the site and to the same workers three or four times. There are all the elements that have been outlined as the model within *The Rayon Spinners*: historical contextualisation, voiced accounts, verbatim comments, multiple methods, observation and generally 'hanging around', and there is the necessary evaluation and theorising to attempt to make sense of these accounts. Again, Ramaswamy's account will be returned to throughout this volume to illustrate the utility of ethnography for industrial relations.

In summary therefore, with some obvious exceptions, ethnography within industrial relations research in the developing world is identified as a significant gap in the field and there are concerning trends that in the developed world, the direction for academic research is moving away from voiced accounts towards more quantitative paradigms. Given the more recent concerns within the development area for voiced accounts, the benefits of ethnographic study in terms of understanding and theorising and the pedigree of ethnographic anthropological work which can be drawn upon, now seems the right time for a new paradigm of industrial relations research to be utilised. Examples from accounts such as those discussed above, plus the West Midlands lock ethnography will be utilised throughout this volume as signposts towards a different way of looking at industrial relations research and analysis.

Plan of the Volume

Having laid the background for an industrial relations analysis which uses ethnographic methods in Chapter One, the main substance of the volume falls into the four remaining chapters. There is a dual purpose in the chapter design that we have chosen. Firstly, Chapters Two, Three and Four deal primarily with different actors within the employment relationship. Chapter Two draws on employee perceptions and attitudes towards management within a workplace context (the actor as manager), Chapter Three draws on perceptions and attitudes amongst the workforce towards each other (the actor as worker/employee), while Chapter Four deals primarily with attitudes and perceptions of the trade union (the actor as trade union activist).

Secondly, the chapters are split thematically, each chapter drawing out from the original lock studies, a particularly important feature of industrial relations, which emerged out of the ethnographic methodology. It is also interesting to note that these themes or features also happen to be areas of neglect within conventional industrial relations studies and which benefit from the analysis allowed by ethnographic methods.

In Chapter Two, we uncover the 'drama of paternalism' which was apparent within the lock ethnographies. Here, we explore the impact of managerial style on industrial relations. In particular, we look at the way in which past traditions of management style inform the expectations and experiences of contemporary employees. In essence, we argue that historical legacies have important implications for the success or failure of present and future management initiatives in any particular workplace context. At the lock companies, this past legacy happened to involve paternalistic management style. We use such a discussion with reference to the developing world to indicate how a need to manage the past as well as the present is a key feature of most industrial relations contexts. We also link our discussion to developing world studies that have a similar concern for the importance of deeply embedded experiences, informed by wider family and community influences.

In Chapter Three we deepen the analysis drawn from Chapter Two by showing the interconnection between historical legacy and embedded experience and gender and family dimensions. Gender and family relations built up over a period of time are seen as very important as a structuring principle of contemporary industrial relations. Thus we add another drama, that of gender and family, as denoting particular scripts and roles deemed appropriate by the lock workforce, which define the interactions between workers and the jobs that they do, and also the response of the workforce to particular restructuring programmes initiated by management. We offer a critique of the neglect of gender and family perspectives within conventional industrial relations and discuss the dangers of such neglect when looking at developing world industrial relations. Conventional industrial relations accounts tend to either be gender invisible or base analysis on gender stereotypes, which ethnographic studies indicate clearly are misplaced, or which do not fully consider the context and web of social interactions in which industrial relations takes place. Most importantly, they do not acknowledge the different and similar experiences of men and women at work and risk leaving millions of women workers unvoiced in the industrial relations accounts.

Chapter Four introduces two interconnected dramas of the employment relationship, the 'drama of negotiation' and the 'drama of collective action'. Here the analysis of the foregoing chapters is deepened still further by using them as a context in which union representatives/activists or leaders engage with both management for the purposes of negotiation and bargaining, and with the workforce, in trying to mobilise and maintain collective support. Such issues are core themes within conventional industrial relations research, however, the ethnographic approach offers new dimensions to such analysis, looking closely at the processes of negotiation and collective action within specific workplace contexts; a current gap in the field. We contend that overall, successful mobilisation of collective support requires the industrial relations actors involved to 'play out' the appropriate role within the expected drama. We discuss the important role that trade unions and collective organisations and movements play in the developing world, but recognise, that worldwide, such movements are currently working within a climate of adversity. In looking at how such organisations might sustain and mobilise participants, we illustrate how ethnographic methods draw out more valuable insights into successful strategies for renewal.

We conclude the book with Chapter Five, in which the key themes of the volume are summarised. We reiterate our contention about the importance of ethnographic methods to the study of industrial relations in the developing world and begin to suggest appropriate directions for future research. In particular, we make some tentative assertions about the way in which new information technologies might impact upon the social relations of, and research into, industrial relations. It is noted that ethnographic study holds its own weaknesses and difficulties, but that these are not insurmountable and in addition, we emphasise that one methodological approach should not take precedence over another. Ethnographically based research can complement, support and challenge the analysis emerging from more conventional industrial relations study.

Chapter Two

Paternalism: Industrial Relations and Historical Legacies[1]

> I remember, it was the early sixties and we were celebrating the centenary of KeyCo. So they organised this trip to Coventry theatre, a show with Mike Yarwood and singing groups for all the employees. There was a huge armada of KeyCo coaches for fifteen hundred of us. And we all went there, and the Managing Director at that time ... he got up onto the platform to give the welcome and there was a huge roar, a standing ovation from all the employees ... It was a real feeling of belonging. You wouldn't get that now do you know what I mean? ... I certainly felt that at that time, that celebration, that warmth that there was towards that man (KeyCo employee, 40 years service).

In this chapter, we explore the impact of managerial style on industrial relations. In particular, we look at the way in which past traditions of management style inform the expectations and experiences of contemporary employees. In essence, we argue that historical legacies have important implications for the success or failure of present and future management initiatives in any particular workplace context.

Paternalism: a Conventional Account

There can be no doubt that paternalism as a management style and expected behaviour of management by employees was an important determinant of the industrial relations context at the lock companies. However, it is through ethnographic enquiry that the real significance of paternalism as a traditional management style emerges as a key determinant of industrial relations. A conventional (quantitative) industrial relations methodology certainly would not have uncovered the importance of paternalism as a structuring principle for the lock factories. The use of ethnographic methods within the lock cases illustrates clearly that the concept of paternalism remains highly relevant to comprehending the change process at such deeply rooted contemporary organisations.

Some background discussion of the concept of paternalism is necessary to illustrate its importance within these particular workplace contexts. Paternalism has been widely observed as a characteristic of (relatively) traditional employment relationships in both rural and industrial societies. Certainly, paternalism has often been used as a way to explain working-class values and behaviour in a variety of settings (Wray, 1996; Warde, 1992). One can see the plurality of its use, for example, from analysis of plantation labour relations in Brazil (Siegel, 1955), to later Victorian factory life (Joyce, 1980; Drummond, 1995) to contemporary debates about human resource management and corporate culture (Legge, 1995).

The *Encyclopedia of the Social Sciences,* states that the root meaning of paternalism derives from a Latin-English kinship term meaning 'a type of behaviour by a superior toward an inferior resembling that of a male parent to his child-in most cases, a son' (Bennett, 1968, p. 472). It should be noted however, that 'the precise forms of [paternalist] behaviour vary from society to society because the culture of kinship varies'. The significance of this variation with regard to the developing world will be discussed in detail later in this chapter. In the context of the lock companies, in line with the root meaning, paternalistic management styles are essentially patriarchal and gendered, the significance of which will be discussed in depth in Chapter Three. However, in relevance to this chapter, we concentrate on the general characteristics, functions and modes of action connected with paternalism.

Whether one is looking at paternalism within colonial plantation systems and other pre-industrial labour systems, paternalism at the turn of the industrial revolution, or contemporary examples, some essential features can be identified. Notably, the managerial element involves taking on responsibilities for workers over and beyond basic contractual provisions for wages and routine working conditions. These responsibilities might involve various benefits including economic resources (such as financial protection and guarantees for the welfare of the worker and his family), basic services and supplies, housing, social facilities and recreational outlets. In return workers are expected to remain with the employer and exhibit loyalty to the firm (Bennett, 1968). Overall, characteristic features of paternalistic organisations thus have tended to include:

> hereditary family ownership, personal relations between employer and workers, a sense of religious mission and a commitment to social welfare and public service. The ideal type paternalist workforce matches these, with family employment through large kinship networks, which are embedded in a surrounding occupational community (Ackers, 1998, pp. 176–7).

However, conventional analysis of paternalism suffers from a variety of weaknesses. Firstly it tends to be utilised in a generalised and imprecise way. Thompson (1993, p. 24) criticises the use of paternalism on a societal scale, for example, characterising Victorian society as a paternalist era, while Warde (1992, p. 702) complains about the lack of detailed analysis about the different types of paternalism which exist. In other words, the use of the concept is not often sufficiently situated in the micro context, or unpacked, so as to see subtle differences in the experience of paternalism. Thus, the concept has become so imprecise and incoherent in usage, it has lost much of its use as an analytical tool (Hobsbawm and Ranger, 1992).

This also serves as a reason for the second weakness of conventional analyses of paternalism; that paternalism is overly criticised as a tool of oppression and exploitation of the working class and is subsequently seen as irrelevant to modern industrial life. Paternalism is often portrayed as an outdated concept, anachronistic in its view of the employment relationship and something to be seen as a detrimental set of practices which belong to a time long since past (Ackers, 1998). In this regard there appear to be inconsistencies within accounts. The *Encyclopaedia of Social Sciences*, in a general way, traces the demise of paternalist forms in various contexts as an inevitable consequence of processes of modernisation bringing with it, social systems stressing individualism and free contract (Bennett, 1968). However this account also recognises cases where, despite economic modernisation and social democratisation, forms of paternalism and the requisite familial models survive indefinitely. While it is stated that the survival or creation of a paternalist system depends on needs and existing social organisational patterns and traditions, there is not the space within such a generalised account to offer a detailed exploration of these needs and patterns and traditions. More recent analysis has called for accounts that firmly situate paternalism within a specific workplace context:

> paternalism is not a general recipe for working-class subordination, but a hypothesis to be tested within a specific workplace and locality during a given historical period (Ackers, 1998, p. 187).

Such a view encourages differences to be drawn out of the practice of paternalism in different cases. More significantly it directs research to highlight differences in the experience of paternalism, from the point of view of managers and workers to be drawn out, so that accounts are properly voiced. This is the utility of the ethnographic method: allowing us to glimpse the specificity of the importance of paternalism within any social situation. Such is the case within the lock firms.

Paternalism at the Lock Companies

The lock companies share many of the characteristic features of paternalism described above. Firstly, employment at the two lock firms is based on a tightly knit, localised work force. Even today, labour turnover is very low, and a high proportion of employees have more than 10 years service, demonstrated in the fact that people who had been involved in the research from its beginnings in the early 1980s were able to be interviewed in 1997. Large complex family networks still exist on the shopfloor, with children following their parents into the industry and the company. The majority of those workers talked to had family members or relatives working in the lock industry; only two people did not have relatives in the firm, and many had immediate family members working with them, including the meeting of spouses in the firm. As one recent retiree stated:

> I'm the third or fourth generation coming into the industry from my mother's side. In fact, the day I left I think I said goodbye to something like a hundred and forty seven years of continuous service.

Many employees still live in Willenhall, and many within walking distance of the factories, reinforcing the sense of occupational community. Some have moved away, indeed while over half of those we talked to in 1983 lived in Willenhall, this had reduced to a quarter of the group by 1996. However the furthest that people lived away from the factory was six miles. This was a close knit occupational community.

Wider Community Influence

A central characteristic of paternalistic management styles is wider company influence in the community (Ackers, 1998, pp. 178–80). Some of these features continue to characterise LockCo and KeyCo. Under family ownership, the companies practised a brand of 'paternalistic capitalism' (Ackers and Black, 1991) which has left a mark on the culture of the modern firms. While formal family ownership ended in the 1960s, all the evidence indicates that the firms continued to be run as 'family firms' with the social fabric of paternalism largely intact. Traditionally, company directors at both firms were well known in the town and factories and frequently enjoyed first name personal relations with workers, a fact remembered nostalgically by many long service employees (Greene, 1999). The perception of the positive influence of a family atmosphere comes through clearly in the employees' descriptions of past company events. One such example is recounted at the beginning of this chapter where a KeyCo employee talks about a company outing to Coventry in the 1960s.

For decades the companies have been at the heart of the local community, including involvement with a wide variety of social and welfare activities such as sports teams, charity sponsorship, company days out and social clubs. Walking around the now defunct clubhouse of the LockCo Sports and Social club on the factory grounds, the walls are strewn with photographs attesting to the company's involvement; the victorious LockCo football team of 1953, or the managing director presenting the winning shield to the champions of the inter-firm bowls tournament in 1972. In a similar way, KeyCo was well known for its social club. This had been a local centre of leisure and sporting activities, parties for children and summer barbecues. This paternalistic style was supported structurally by a general tradition of low labour turnover; a high proportion of long service employees; and large, complex family networks. Management helped to sustain this by working with the industrial trade union (National Union of Lock and Metal Workers) to avoid forced redundancies through methods of short time working, voluntary redundancies, transfer of employees around the factory and by the use of the pool of labour in the form of relations and family members through a form of 'extended internal labour market' (Manwaring, 1984).[2] It should be noted that by the late 1990s, more people had joined the company through alternative avenues than this informal family route than in earlier studies, suggesting the decline of this family tradition. Regardless, the legacy of the family firm atmosphere loomed large in the discourse of those workers spoken to.

The Human Face of Paternalism

Another feature of paternalism is its personal and face to face nature:

> Paternalism, in whatever shape or form, depends for its efficacy on the 'human element', on some sense of the visible human hand, however simulated, in lieu of impersonal economic forces (Ackers, 1998, pp. 185–7).

At KeyCo until the takeover in 1988 and at LockCo until the merger in 1997, the same traditional management hierarchy had existed for decades. This hierarchy was heavily vertically differentiated, both by job title (directors, managers, supervisors, superintendent, foremen, chargehand) but also physically on the shopfloor by use of uniforms. There was a tradition by which managers would work their way up from the shopfloor. In 1987, 90 per cent of foremen and two-thirds of supervisors and virtually all superintendents at LockCo had been promoted from the shopfloor. In LockCo, the managing director before the merger had originally worked in the time study department. At one of the joint union/management meetings attended, we observed how a retired assembly line worker had addressed this managing director by his first name because she had known him as a small child. Feelings of family firm atmosphere, and close, personal contact with management, matching a paternalistic culture, infuse the discourse of those employees spoken to. Some talked about their memories of the old family managers and their caring attitude towards the employees:

> well when I went there first, there was two LockCo brothers, ... but they were a very paternal people. I wouldn't say that the wages were the highest or anything like that but if you had any difficulties, financial or family, they'd help you out if you went to see them, they really would, even though it was a fair sized company, they really would help people out.

KeyCo employees reminisced similarly about the close personal contact they used to have with the family management: As one worker related, 'years ago with the old management they'd come down on the shopfloor and have a chat with you, have a laugh and a joke, but not now, no, all that's gone'. Others commented similarly, 'Well at one time, if the gaffer come in, he'd walk round, say hello, shake your hand' and, '... managers always used to come around, walk through the shop, the old MD used to start at one end and walk through the shop every morning'.

All Change at the Lock Companies

In understanding industrial relations and the relational processes which we observed and heard about occurring in the late 1990s, the collective memory of workers at the lock companies and the expectations of present management which developed from these memories are key to an understanding of the contemporary situation. Certainly, much has changed over the period since the new firm has taken over and merged the two firms. The new owners have essentially attempted radical modernisation, effectively sweeping away decades of workplace custom and traditional work organisation on the shopfloor. Policies over the 1990s included the introduction of new technology and cellular work organisation, the abolition of piecework and its replacement by cashless measured day work and a productivity-based bonus scheme. There was evidence within management rhetoric of a desire to get the company working as a team, a focus on customer service, and a need to break down traditional 'them and us' attitudes. Management discourse reflected the objective of changing the conditions of the relationship between management and employees in order to elicit greater commitment and work effort, evoking the rhetoric of human resource management (HRM) (Grant, 1996).

In addition, as part of the restructuring at both of the firms, the traditional management hierarchy had changed significantly. At lower levels, the traditional charge hand and foreman positions had been abolished. Each team or cell had an appointed team leader or 'Grade Two', all of whom were promoted from the shopfloor. Middle management had been significantly thinned and there was now a group of line managers, was created, many of whom were new to the job, although the majority were promoted from the shopfloor. At senior level, there was an almost total change of departmental managers and directors. As the Personnel Director in 1996 at KeyCo stated:

> every senior vacancy that occurred, we went outside to fill, with the objective that bringing in business management expertise rather than lock expertise … We changed I suspect about half the managers.

Overall, therefore, there was an influx of new, young, professional managers, many of them graduates from outside of the lock industry. All the managers who had been promoted from shopfloor level, and who had a familiarity with the lock-making culture of the town, were replaced. The way in which managerial practice was at odds with that expected by the workforces at the two companies, became clearly apparent.

Paternalism: an Ethnographic Account

The significance of the above changes however, is in the impact that they had on the views and perceptions of the employment relationship and consequently on the success of the new owners in changing the culture of the firms and ultimately increasing profit. Any quantitative survey could have easily demonstrated the ostensible success or failure of the restructuring process to meet management aims in achieving productivity gains, while an attitude survey may have indicated some basic assessment of the company's success in winning the 'hearts and minds' of employees. Such an analysis would probably have indicated that the restructuring achieved some of the primary aims. KeyCo was producing more efficiently and there were some upturns in profit margins. Customer service had improved, and company statistics indicated that most departments had a reached a 90 per cent customer service record; a vast improvement on that before the restructuring programmes. However, what more in-depth ethnographic methods allow us to explore, are the complexities of these facts and figures, and how they are lived out in experience. More importantly, they offer some possible explanations for why the restructuring had the effects that it did.

Rhetoric Versus Reality

There were obviously serious deficiencies in the process of restructuring. While there were some nominal gains, the product targets set by management were largely not achieved and KeyCo was certainly not making the profits that were expected by management. One indicator of this was the fact that a bonus payment, paid on the level of finished goods into the warehouse, was not triggered once since it had been in place. This was of great concern to the managers, who were very disappointed in the disparity of success that different teams were having in meeting targets, and were aware of the detrimental affect that this was having on motivation on the shopfloor:

> If we get the bonus to start paying out then I think people will realise the company is doing better ... and they're actually getting the benefit from it, ... but I think it's important that over this period we actually start seeing the bonus trigger ... you look round and you know that some people in some areas have worked hard and they've got nothing to show for it and that is like kind of discouraging (factory manager).

Certainly this manager's views were confirmed by those of the workers. Most employees were very unhappy about the bonus scheme, believing that it meant that they were expected to work harder for less money. There was a general sense of disappointment that the system had not yet triggered a bonus payment and there seemed little optimism that it would in the future. This was seen as a large disincentive to working harder and is one explanation for the falling effort levels testified to by product targets not being met. As one shopfloor worker at KeyCo commented: 'There's no incentive to really push ... however hard people work, there's nothing there at the end of the month.' Despite many people remarking on the increased demands that management made for them to increase their effort, the majority of employees admitted that their workload had lessened and that their effort had decreased. While many commented that they had originally worked harder in order to get the bonus payments promised, over time, the lack of incentive from measured day work and the failure of the bonus system had led to employees withdrawing extra effort. Workers at KeyCo spoke of the establishment of an equity value of work effort where individuals were concerned to only work as hard as the person next to them or the people in their team because they all receive the same wage:

> People have worked harder and harder, and there's no bonus at the end of the month ... so why break your back if you're getting paid the same.

> I've found myself slowing down because I look up the shop and there's people ... having the time of their lives, and you think, what the hell am I doing, I'm working away and ... she's earning as much money as me.

We were at LockCo before and during the restructuring process and could compare this with the completed restructuring context at KeyCo. As ethnographic observers, one of the main noticeable differences was the working pace. Conditions were certainly hard at the factory before the restructuring. The most prominent image of work on the shopfloor, particularly that done by the women (the piece workers) was its extremely fast pace. Everywhere was activity. There was a noticeable difference after the restructuring. Certainly, housekeeping conditions on the shopfloor of both firms had improved dramatically, at least from a cosmetic viewpoint. The factory floor was tidier, with much more space between machine lines. Assembly work was still fast, but noticeably less frantic. What was most illuminating however, was the amount of people chatting, standing around, smoking and congregating at the drinks machine. People were working less, there could be no doubt. Not only did employees say that they were working less, this was also corroborated by the physical comparison before and after by an outside observer.

Managers were largely of the view that the restructuring was only of benefit to workers, allowing them to work cooperatively, fostering team spirit and taking away the pressure of piecework. They also pointed out that financially, most workers had benefited from the new work organisation, indeed only a very small percentage of the workforce (those with the highest piecework rates) had lower wages after the abolition of piecework. Thus, an explanation based around material concerns, is obviously not sufficient for understanding falling effort rates.

The Deconstruction of Paternalist Exchange

As an alternative explanation, discussion with workers leads us to explore the break down of the social relations of paternalism. A vehement negativity towards management was voiced by all of the workers at both companies that we spoke to. Comments focused around the dismantling of various elements of paternalism which had been progressing since the early 1980s and which was exacerbated by the recent takeover and merger. Here ethnographic methods allowed us to identify two aspects of paternalism, which stand out as particularly salient in helping to understand situation. First, a need to recognise the importance of the 'human element' to paternalism and second, that paternalism involves a balance of coercion and consent, and is implicitly a reciprocal relationship.

Dismantling of the human element There was a lot of similarity between the attitudes found at both lock companies. The general view of management was negative, with employees assessing the conduct of their managers on the basis of similar criteria; namely the deterioration in the level of contact with managers on the shopfloor and lack of concern for the welfare of the workforce. One of the main criteria on which managers appeared to be judged by employees was the issue of contact, accessibility and communication. Comparison over the whole period 1983–97 at LockCo finds that views of the level of contact demonstrated employees' overall feelings of disappointment in the distance and separation between employees and top management. Most in 1997 stated that they had little or no contact with managers above superintendent level, reflected in comments such as, 'you say good morning to them and things like that, but you don't sort of have conversations really', while some commented specifically that there was a feeling of separation and distance between managers and employees, reflective of an overall feeling of 'them and us'. In general, the impression is that there was little contact between employees and managers, especially at top level, where any contact is fleeting and superficial, for example, 'Sometimes you get the odd handshake at Christmas and that's it for the year. Very superficial.'

The general tone of the negative attitudes towards management at KeyCo was very similar to that at LockCo. Typical comments included: '… they never come round to see us, they walk around, look at the place and tut and walk off,' and 'management don't bother you at all. Until something goes wrong, they don't know you.' Another added, 'they come in and they don't even introduce themselves ... you should get to know people surely'.

The general sense of a lack of contact and of separation is interesting bearing in mind that many people at KeyCo felt that the amount of communication had increased in the last two years. Indeed the rhetoric of the new KeyCo management placed a great emphasis on the need for improved communication between managers and employees. People remarked on the new communication devices that had been introduced such as, team briefings, monthly meetings, and newsletters. However, the discourse did not suggest that the channels which exist for communication between employees and managers are leading to an open culture, indeed very few felt that such meetings were useful or interesting. Most remarked that much information was circulated by rumour and hearsay. One person commented that they heard about developments too late to have any opportunity to contribute. Others commented that while communication channels were in place, employees were not using them properly. In general, most employees were not satisfied with the nature of company communication that existed, because they did not feel they could contribute, and because they still did not receive a sufficient amount of information.

The majority of the group did not see KeyCo as an open organisation and most commented on the lack of freedom that existed to voice their feelings and views to management. The main reason cited for this lack of freedom, was fear and insecurity about their jobs. Many people believed that speaking out would result in severe recriminations by 'being branded a negative thinker'. Instead, people kept their opinions to themselves and only made suggestions in private to other employees, seen in remarks such as: 'after the meetings people come back and say what they think but they won't with management there, they're afraid for their jobs', and 'if you have a negative attitude, you don't know what kind of impact that has if there are redundancies or something, so I tend to falsely agree with them'.

One example of this was related to us by a number of people including a manager and which had almost become like a folk tale (Gabriel, 2000) on the shopfloor. Parts for machining and assembly were kept in boxes alongside those people working with them. This incident involved a box of springs, which normally would be separated by layers of paper to prevent the springs becoming entwined with each other. However, this made them difficult to handle quickly and so on this occasion, the employee had laid them all out on the bench next to him. When the new Operations Director came through the shopfloor, he noticed that these springs were not put away tidily and in an effort to maintain housekeeping discipline had told the employee to put them back in the box. Following these instructions to the letter, this employee threw them all back in the box so that when somebody needed to use some springs, they were all tangled up. When the team leader questioned the employee, he answered that he had simply done what the manager had told him to do. When we asked the storytellers for explanations of this incident, responses varied from being due to a situation where workers do not feel that they can offer suggestions or alternatives to managers, to the fact that the relationship is such that the worker saw this an act of defiance to management, knowing full well that it was the wrong thing to do. Either way, a lack of communication was demonstrated, and when we asked one of the employees why they felt this incident had arisen, they remarked, 'it's still them and us isn't it'.

Dismantling of reciprocity Ethnographic enquiry allows us to see the ambiguities, and contradictions in practice, and offers explanations by highlighting the importance of paternalism as a necessarily two-way and reciprocal relationship. The owners proclaimed the new 'open' atmosphere of the companies and at the new KeyCo team briefings, managers clearly proclaimed aspirations to involve employees and break down communication barriers. However, in private conversation, most of the managers did not seem convinced of the two way nature of the communication process and indeed did not see this as a priority issue. As the Operations Director stated: 'There was very little leeway for a two way process. The communication has been very much ... one way.' The Engineering Manager commented similarly that: 'Oh absolutely, they are imposed from above, because at the end of the day we hope that what we're ... doing are good common sense ideas.' Finally, the Chief Accountant stated: 'It has to be imposed, there has to be a degree of contempt but having said that, it's good for them, you don't realise what's good for you until it's happened.' Management discourse thus evoked a condescending, authoritarian attitude towards the workforce, where 'they know best'.

Reinforcing this, conversations with workers at both firms suggested that there was a general view of separation in terms of contact, between the shopfloor and management. Additionally, a vocabulary of 'them and us' and views of a degree of separation between managers and employees were apparent in both 1996 and 1983 at LockCo, but there does appear to be an increase in such feelings across the period. As LockCo employees related:

> there's a definite gulf between the top and the work force, it's like a them and us situation.. and they seem to want to keep it in that vein.
>
> I think they're stuck up really. I mean it takes them all their time … just to say a word of 'Good Morning', they just look as if to say 'You're lower down than what I am'.
>
> It's them and us, that's all it is. If they want favours doing, they're all smiles and when everything running right and you want a favour doing, they don't want to know. You know you can take a chap off the shopfloor and put him in a suit and his attitude turns straight away.
>
> Management are different to us you know, we're the workers, you do what they tell you to do, so they're above you. It's like when you were at school really, you've got the teachers and the kids, you know.

At KeyCo, one female packer commented, 'They sort of walk around thinking "I'm it, you're shite." I mean they don't speak to the people on the shopfloor, they totally ignore us.' This feeling was also apparent in views that they were treated like children by management: 'well you don't treat school kids like they do we. It's like you're in a Borstal or something, the way they come round, their attitude to we …' and, 'they could start treating us like adults instead of children. You can't talk to them like one human being to another.'

The historical legacy also becomes important, however. Employees at both firms compared their present managers with the family management of the past. As one woman at LockCo stated, 'top management don't talk to people whereas they used to when I started here, it was more like a family', while another added:

> When I first started you had your own directors and they used to come round and say good morning to you. They knew your name but all that's gone now. You rarely see anybody.

Some commented about their memories of the old family managers and their caring attitude towards the employees:

> At one time they were a bit more lenient … I can remember at one time, a girl went up and went part time because she had to look after her Dad … and they let her go part time, but I can't see them even considering that now …

Another remarked:

> I mean under the LockCo regime, the brothers, I know one or two people who've been stuck financially and they've spoken to them and they helped them out. This lot wouldn't, they wouldn't even throw you a life belt if you was drowning.

Employees felt that the relationship between managers and employees had become more formalised over the years. As one man said in 1997:

> You have to go through the right channels now ... I mean I could be sitting next to a manager ... and all I'd have to do was tell him what I wanted to tell him, but you know, now it's tended to be a lot more formal.

Another added:

> The relationship between management and employees had become more fragmented, there'd been more managerial positions made. I mean in the older days, the manager used to do many different occupations but later on there was personnel manager, with a staff which meant that there had to be an assistant personnel manager, and it progressed.

This was seen as a particular problem for the trade union shop stewards who felt that the personal relationships had declined, where they could just knock on a manager's door and deal with a problem, whereas now, more had to be put on paper and proper procedure had to be followed. As one ex-steward remarked:

> the shop steward should have the right ... to go straight to Personnel and start talking now there's more failures to agree have to be registered to get anywhere, even on small things you'd never heard of them before ... because it would nearly always be sorted out but now management won't talk to you.

The increasing formality and distance of the relationship was seen as a clear impediment to 'getting things done'.

Employees at both firms in 1997 also commented on the decline of company involvement in the local community. People at LockCo related this in a similar way to their nostalgia about contact with managers:

> We had a sports facility, football, bowls, tennis, good repartee with the management and everything. It's all gone. The sports fields gone, the bowling has gone, the tennis has gone, everything has gone. I think that sort of thing keeps a company together. They used to have two/three football teams here, they have a job to find one now. Because they ain't got the heart in the company,

> in my opinion. This ain't the company I started at forty years ago. It's like an alien to me now.

A worker at KeyCo spoke in a similar vein:

> they have downgraded and not invested in the social part of the company at all. The sports club has never been improved, in fact it's closed down. The internal sports facilities and teams have been run down.

> The employer tended to drop out of that sort of thing, the sports and all that, they're not interested in that side of things.

The proposed closure of the LockCo Social Club was an issue raised at a shop steward's committee meeting.[3] The Social Club had as long a history as the company, providing a place on the factory site where employees could meet socially and providing facilities for a wide variety of sports. Indeed, the original company handbook had prided itself on the company sports teams. This was held up as another sign of the lack of company concern with the welfare of the workforce and there was support from the committee for a campaign to save the club. However, the closure did proceed and the club premises are now only used to hold union meetings in. In a similar way, the company also announced the closing of the Locks Welfare Society.[4] This had existed for 80 years and which, with company administrative support, was run by a joint committee of managers and workers and funded by a weekly payment by members from their wages. Its role was to provide financial assistance to members in cases of illness and various social functions such as annual parties for retirees. The trade union has since taken over the administrative running of the society from the company.

Similarly, there has been a lapsing of the Long Service Dinners over the period when they had been held up as a major event of the company's calendar. The commemorative booklet for the dinner in December 1982 notes that 160 people attended, of whom 37 people were celebrating over 40 years service, 75 were celebrating over 30 years service and 78 had been at the firm over 25 years. This was an impressive account of the many years people had spent at the firm and which appears to have died out by the 1990s, even though there were still many long service employees.

Any involvement that still existed therefore, only served to highlight the lack of perks and goodwill given to employees by management. Company involvement was not seen to reflect the caring involvement of the past where employees remembered the annual work's dance, children's Christmas parties, company sports teams, pensioner's events and 'Christmas boxes'. One man was particularly disappointed that management refused to support and sponsor a KeyCo football team when he had made a proposal in 1995. He felt that they were missing out on any company loyalty that was left: 'I mean at the end of the day we work at KeyCo and we want to promote KeyCo. Something like that, it's nothing ... For such a big firm, you'd think they could do more in the local community.' Many stated specifically that they thought that the company should have more of a social and welfare role in the community, as one woman at KeyCo remarked: 'They build relationships, it's what makes the company tick, makes a company a company and not a them and us.' Overall, therefore, at both firms, there has been a significant decline in the level of company involvement over the period.

The Need to Play the Part

In some respects, such a separation between the shopfloor and management, feelings of 'them and us', and 'father knows best' decision-making processes are what might be expected within a traditional, paternalistic culture. In line with such a viewpoint, employees did not want to challenge the managerial prerogative to manage. The feelings of 'them and us' in the company were seen as an inevitable part of factory life and did not necessarily mean that workers and managers were always in conflict with one another. As one female expediter commented:

> I don't think it's management against employees, it's just the way it's always been. I don't think they're against we, and they're only out for themselves or we wouldn't have got half of what we've got, but it's always been them and us.

In a similar way, another said, 'I wouldn't say it's them and us, I wouldn't say we was completely dead against each other.' On the other hand, while there were some indications of an acceptance of the status quo, the views of disappointment with the degree of separation are significant within the specific lock industry context, with its traditions of a family-based, paternalistic management style.

It is worth emphasising the reciprocal nature of paternalism as a management style. Drawing on Drummond (1994) it is important to recognise how neither deference nor dependence alone explain the paternalist relationship; there is a complex mix of reciprocal rights and duties for both parties to the relationship. Thus while new management practice continued to evoke paternalistic authority, managers were not prepared to take on the expected reciprocal duties of paternalistic authority relations, as indicated by the concerns about personal contact. In addition, there was a view from the new managers that traditions of any kind should be positively discouraged as an obstacle to change. In particular, most of the management team were negative, and in some cases extremely contemptuous of the historical traditions that existed within the firm, which they saw as old-fashioned and out-of-date. One comment typified the views of most of the management team:

> Oh yes, they exist all right. I still cringe when I come across them ... having been involved in the industry for twenty or thirty years is becoming increasingly irrelevant.

There was a general view that rather than the history and traditions being a positive feature of the company, the existence of family networks and long service was 'incestuous', and a 'force for stasis'.

The significance of this discussion is in looking at the effect of this lack of recognition of the importance of the deeply embedded traditional practices and attitudes. For example, while the new production and payment systems did not directly attack paternalism, there was a significant indirect effect. The economistic emphasis within HRM of labour as a resource appears to clash with the social relationship of paternalism (Bacon and Storey, 1996). In essence, management had attempted to end a particular culture, which had been internalised over generations. This 'way of working' had represented a workplace culture and a framework for workplace relations. Piecework had been more than just a payment system; it had been a 'way of life' (Sennett, 1998).

Equally, despite the generally negative tone of feelings towards management, there was an impression of underlying (albeit declining) commitment to the lock companies. Many employees voiced a willingness to put in effort to make the company successful and expressed feelings of company loyalty. In some cases, this pride was seen to relate to the brand name. As one KeyCo employee commented:

> [KeyCo] is a well known company, if you go in hardware shops, or do-it-yourself shops you always see [KeyCo] so I feel quite proud to be part of that company really ... whereas you might be working for somebody who's got a bad reputation.

Another shopfloor worker added:

> Well it's got a very good name everywhere you go, when you talk about locks, the first thing people say is [KeyCo]. I think that's good and I think the company ought to realise that.

One man commented specifically about the pride that they had in making a good product and how this had declined:

> Oh absolutely, we try the best to make a good standard of [product], I think the way the company's going, we're losing that, which is a shame really, it's a shame it's getting this way, to lose that genuine pride down there.

What was particularly evident from workers' discussions was a degree of underlying affectionate feeling for the lock firms. People seemed genuinely unhappy that the place did not hold the same atmosphere any longer. One man ruefully remarked that LockCo was 'like an alien to me now'. It is not surprising that people felt similarly bearing in mind the fact that many people had invested most of their adult lives in LockCo. In fact, given the vulnerability of their situation as employees, the uncomfortable conditions, gruelling pace of work and deterioration in company atmosphere, what is more surprising is how common were feelings that people enjoyed coming to work. For many people, work was a sociable place, as one machinist commented:

> I got into a crowd and they made me feel that welcome, and you sit in a group sort of thing, and we had that many laughs and that much fun, it weren't like coming to work, it was a pleasure.

While she felt that the atmosphere had declined over the period, she was still able to state that, 'even though it's only a factory I love my job, I love the work, I love coming to work'. Working at the factory had become a firm part of most employees' lives, indeed talking to one retiree highlighted this point as he felt that there was very little left in his life now that he'd left LockCo. As he related:

> I miss talking to the chaps, football talk on a Monday morning … I've really lost the ability to enjoy myself, I really have. I know it sounds funny but I went on holiday and I didn't know what to do, I was bored senseless most of the time. The only thing I really look forward to is a drink down the pub.

Despite the deterioration in relations on the shopfloor between managers and workers, there was still a very strong impression that the company was viewed as a community asset and a local social institution. For many people, the lock companies *were* Willenhall. This was a view that local press and union newsletters frequently drew upon, pointing out that the survival of the lock firms was imperative for the survival of the town itself and its local community.

This reflected a widespread, underlying affection for the companies and working at the firms pervaded the discourse of workers. There was a general feeling that people wanted to return to a situation where they could feel proud of where they worked, as one machinist remarked: 'I'd like to enjoy working for KeyCo again … I'd like it to get back to the way it was.' Working at the lock companies had been a part of most of their adult lives and as one person typically remarked: 'I've always loved KeyCo, I wouldn't have worked here twenty-five years if I didn't would I? It's always been a comfort to come here.' People were genuinely unhappy about the decline in the atmosphere of the firm and the fact that they no longer enjoyed coming to work. A typical comment included:

> It used to be a happy-go-lucky place at one time, but not now.

> Now it's just dog eat dog, the social atmosphere is gone … at one time you used to come into work in the morning, you used to hear people whistling, but now you think 'Oh God, I've got to go to that place again'.

This decline in company loyalty and pride over the years had some consequences in terms of work effort. One packer at KeyCo related an incident that occurred in the mid-1980s, soon after she had started at the company, when people had stayed behind hours after work in order to meet a contract they were behind schedule on. Her view was that the reputation of the firm was at stake. The promise to the customer had to be met. The contemporary discourse suggested however, that such an incident was much less likely to occur in the 1990s. Now, requests for overtime work were seen in the light of redundancies, arbitrary changes to work organisation and the one sided relationship between managers and employees.

Managers were aware of this traditional support and commitment to the company. As the factory manager remarked on his impression of the workers at KeyCo compared to his old firm:

> they actually talked passionately about KeyCo … and that surprised me so on one hand you get people saying they only come for the money, but it actually runs deeper than that, because I've worked with people who I know are only coming for the money, and there is quite a difference. I mean I don't think you

> feel grievances about mismanagement if you don't care what's happening to the place, you don't feel uptight because you see things in your mind going backwards if you don't care about the place.

However, there did not seem to be much evidence of a managerial desire to tap into this underlying loyalty, or explicit recognition of its existence.

A Need to Manage the Past as Well as the Present

Explanations for the failure of the change process must be set within an historical framework of traditional family paternalism. The past experience of employees was of an authoritarian, yet more personal and friendly employment relationship, where there was significant contact between managers and employees on the shopfloor. In addition, it was one where managers worked their way up through the company from apprentice level, where there were joint decision-making and consultative committees, and where there was a large degree of company welfare involvement, both within the factory walls and in the wider Willenhall community. It was on the basis of these expectations that management were felt to fall short. As Martin and Fryer found with their study of workers at Casterton Mill, these perceptions 'are not only a product of present milieux, but of present milieux interpreted in the light of past experience and expectations for the future' (1975, p. 113). The success of the paternalistic style is related to the social structures and relationships in place within a specific workplace and locality during a given historical period (Ackers, 1998). The failure of the change process to win 'hearts and minds' at the lock companies in the late 1990s, was primarily rooted in the extent to which managers were seen to have neglected to fulfil their traditional paternalist role. The result was an ambivalent shopfloor consciousness, of hostility towards the company standing alongside a more complex discourse of aspirations of cooperation (Ackers and Black, 1992). However, this did not directly threaten the maintenance of overall managerial prerogative. These positive expectations of cooperation and contact did not exclude the general principle that employees and management should occupy separate positions, indeed much of the discourse suggested that this was an accepted inevitability of the 'them and us' view of the employment relationship. This reflects a traditional view of the 'master-servant' nature of a paternalistic employment relationship (Fox, 1985) and many perceptions characteristic of the 'traditional' and 'deferential' worker (Lockwood, 1966).

Paternalism in practice is a delicate balance of coercion and consent. LockCo and KeyCo employees would welcome a return to the more friendly and personal nature of the relationship, within that paternalistic framework, which they perceive existed in the past. It was here that management lost out in the relationship. One might anticipate the positive effects of management and employers meeting the expectations of employees today – as Martin and Fryer stated, 'Deference is fostered by behaviour regarded as appropriate' (1975, p. 112). At the lock companies, this involved personal and particularistic contact, a concern for employee welfare and a wider social responsibility. Employees wanted more cooperation with management and would welcome more communication and participation in the decisions made about their work lives. These attitudes, coupled with the evidence of loyalty to the employer and willingness to go 'out of my way' in order to make the company a success, suggested a potential; as yet, untapped. The mixture of conflict and cooperation that is revealed is characteristic of the employment relationship (Edwards, 1995), where consent, compliance, resistance and conflict are mutually embedded. Collinson (1994, p. 51) found similar elements of ambiguity among the 'Slavs' workers in his study, where even the most critical and radical of workers in the engineering factory, supported managerial prerogative.

What the ethnographies of LockCo and KeyCo demonstrate is just how difficult it is to disembed long-standing traditions of organisational culture (Giddens, 1991, p. 21). In traditional employment settings, workers do not view change as 'rational economic agents' but through a lens of past experience, passed down through generations. In other words, a firm cannot escape the intended and unintended consequences of its past actions. It is important not to romanticise the concept of paternalism and see it as a panacea; it is after all a 'system of control' (Fox, 1985, p. 3) and there are numerous examples of its detrimental effects, especially on the workforce (Drummond, 1994; Rae, 1969). However, the lock workers were very supportive of certain aspects of paternalistic management. What is uncovered here is a 'theatre of paternalism', one aspect of the drama of the employment relationship, where defined roles and scripts are assigned to the various actors.

This is not to imply that management could 'fake' paternalism. Paternalism is about an underlying relationship of reciprocal duties and responsibilities. It is in these terms that management at the lock companies were seen to fall short. Managers were criticised for not fulfilling their expected role in the 'drama' of the paternalism. In this respect, the past has to be managed as well as the present. There was evidence in the discourse of managers that they desired increased employee commitment to the firm, so that a team ethos was created and the 'them and us' feeling reduced. Part of successfully achieving these aims must involve the fulfilment of employee expectations about the nature of the employment relationship. In this particular context, this included some paternalistic elements.

This thus counters the claims of some, that paternalism is outdated and ostensibly detrimental to employees. While paternalism may be seen as an anachronism in certain situations, in these particular contexts, where there are industrial, occupational and community characteristics that are themselves products of past regimes, the consequences of this older style of management have to be considered. The historic traditions are formative of a particular culture at the lock companies, which underpins the employment relationship. Restructuring which takes no cognisance of this stands to destroy this positive potential in the employment relationship.

The Relevance of Paternalism to Developing World Industrial Relations

Social scientists interested in paternalism have given considerable attention to developing world contexts. For example, reaching a fairly pessimistic conclusion about the likelihood of modern developed world businesses building up the material bases of rhetorical support for paternalistic structures and welfare employment policies, Ackers (1998, p. 191) turns to the developing world.

> The developing world, however, with its collision of old and new social relations, may offer more fertile soil, as the post-war Japanese economic miracle has already charted ... businesses in countries where wages and social restrictions are attractively low but whose poor educational and cultural infrastructure militates against the right sort of labour discipline and commitment, may be inclined to domesticate a labour force within a company town sealed off from the rest of society.

Similarly, in her investigation of the impact of paternalism in the Courtaulds silk mills, Judy Lown (1983, p. 44; see Chapter Three in this volume) points to the parallels between her discussions of an occupational community and industrial development in the developing world. In the *Encyclopaedia of Social Sciences*, John Bennett also refers to developing world examples, in particular those of rural plantation paternalism. Siegel (1955) identifies paternalistic relationships within the working contexts of rural Brazil (cowboy and ranch owner, agricultural worker and farmer). Alexander (1962) uses Argentinian plantations as a case example, Beardsley et al. (1959) looks at rural paternalism in Japan, while Sayigh (1958) looks at Lebanon.

We also begin to see hints of similar analysis as indicated in the lock ethnographies, emerging from these developing world studies. Much of Bennett's analysis is based around discussing whether or not social change has led to the disappearance of paternalistic patterns, in line with much of the conventional analysis discussed earlier. Unionisation, legislative protection, state welfare policies and land reform measures are seen as forces for challenge to paternalistic systems of industrial relations, and have been noted to have led to a decline of paternalism in such examples as Guatemala (Adams, 1959) and Japan (Bennett and Ishino, 1963). However Bennett also notes that there has been the surprising resilience or even creation of paternalistic systems within more modern conditions. In Peru, Ford (1953) notes that labour leaders demanded paternalistic practices, while Dutch sugar plantation owners introduced paternalistic systems in line with local traditions (Geertz, 1965). Despite factory industrial relations being based largely on the concept of the labour contract (Bennett, 1968), researchers have noted the appearance of paternalistic relations within factory systems, reflecting wider social structures and practices. Such is the case in Vreeland's (1957) account of Iranian factories, Stein's (1955) study of Brazilian textile factories or the Japanese spinning mills (Abegglen, 1958). The concluding discussion of paternalism in the *Encyclopedia* revolves around the view that while social change might lead to the dismantling of paternalism in some cases, in others, needs and social organisational patterns and traditions might be more fertile ground for paternalism.

Such a discussion hints at the crux of the explanation as it continues 'the memories of suitable forms of paternalism and the requisite familial models, may survive indefinitely' (Bennett, 1968, p. 476). This appears to fit with our views of the drama of paternalist management, built up over many generations, which forms part of the lock workers' expectations today. However, persuasive support for such an argument within Bennett's account is not present, notably because it is an encyclopaedic entry and is much older, but also because the analysis remains unvoiced. We do not hear the voices and experiences of those individuals involved. We do not gain such a rich understanding of the meaning of paternalistic relations as a structuring principle of industrial relations, illuminating the exchange nature of the relationship and highlighting embedded expectations of roles within the employment relationship.

Moving the Debate Forward: Authentic Voices, Authentic Accounts (I)

It is certainly the case that if we are looking for contexts where paternalism is perhaps a more viable or relevant industrial relations style, then workplaces within the developing world may be more fruitful. However, this does not appear to be the most useful way of looking at the analysis. Notably, such a position sustains the binarism between traditional and modern, old and new, developing and developed. In looking at the developing world as 'more fertile soil' for paternalism, Ackers (1998) is not taking advantage of the real value of the comparison. It is not that we are looking for a 'lost world' of paternalism in a developing world context, but that parallels can be drawn between the developing and developed: the lock companies indicate to us quite clearly the importance of historical legacy to contemporary industrial relations. Consequently, the lock ethnographies indicate how difficult it is for management to implement change, without concern for meeting expectations, which derive from deeply embedded social processes and practices. Such conclusions can be drawn in both developed and developing world examples.

Within Ramaswamy's (1994) longitudinal account of a rayon-spinning factory outside of Delhi, a similar emphasis is placed on the importance of traditional industrial relations as influencing contemporary experiences. The overall aim of the study is to investigate whether or not a clearly defined industrial relations strategy was undertaken by both managers and trade unions over a 15 year period of intense qualitative immersion in the workplace context. While the historical legacy of the rayon-spinning firm is of decades rather than centuries, Ramaswamy traces industrial relations processes in the firm back to its origins in the 1950s. The management style of benevolent family paternalism which characterised the firm from the 1950s to 1980s is seen as a key industrial relations determinant, particularly on the role of trade unions within the firm (which will be discussed as a general industrial relations feature in more detail in Chapter Four):

> the family style of management which had dominated the company for two decades left a deep mark on the labour movement, and the trade unions moulded themselves into a shape prescribed by management style and strategy (ibid., p. 26).

In similarity to the lock cases, Ramaswamy also focuses on the impact on industrial relations of a fundamental change in ownership in the 1980s, when the two founding industrialists parted company. This change in ownership coincides with a noticeable breakdown in labour/management relations, which interviews and observation indicate, was partly due to a break down in the contact and communication channels between management and employees. Workers and trade unions no longer had easy access to the managing director who eschewed the personal, family style of management for a more professional, aloof and human resources specialist style. Unlike the previous managing director, the new owner spoke a different language to the workforce and visited the factory infrequently. The responsibility for industrial relations was no longer held by the family patriarch, but professional managers brought in from outside of the firm. The similarity in comparison between this account of an Indian factory and that of the West Midlands lock companies is very striking. While the 'new management was determined to break with the past by moving away from manipulative methods' (Ramaswamy, 1994, p. 156), in a similar way to the new lock owners, there seemed little realisation that this past had to be managed as well as the present. The reciprocal nature of paternalism, which emerges clearly from the lock workers' expectations of the managerial role, is exactly mirrored by the views of the rayon spinners: 'for workers, the redeeming feature of the old management style was the human benevolence of the managing director' (ibid., p. 153).

There are differences in the accounts, as one would expect. Most notably, Ramaswamy does not find in the discourse of the rayon spinners, the same level of underlying loyalty and pride in the firm, which was demonstrated at the lock firms. Ramaswamy does not however offer any theorised explanations for this lack of employee commitment/loyalty. What the lock ethnographies allow is a situating of employee attitudes and viewpoints within a wider framework of social processes involved with family and community, which we discuss in detail in Chapter Three. Such an analysis is not undertaken in Ramaswamy's account, which if conducted, may have uncovered issues of collective, community memory as in the lock cases.

We need to recognise the importance of industries to particular communities. For example, we find similarities in the lock industry in parts of India. As Kulsherethra states: 'Aligarh and its lock industry are synonymous' (1996, p. 87). Industries can 'make' communities. In Aligarh, the lock industry is seen as a significant factor binding the local community together, encouraged by tradition and historical legacy which saw employers, employees and contractors coming from the same community and having been dependent on each other for generations. However, Kulsherethra's account remains unvoiced and so provides only a glimpse of the complex web of social relations which bind the community together.

Summary: Moving Beyond the Contemporary

To reiterate the overall points made within this chapter, ethnographic analysis at the lock companies highlighted the importance of historical legacy, handed down through generations of workers to generate a collective memory of experiences and expectations. We were then able to greater understand the process of restructuring, and its successes and failures in context. For the lock companies, the collective memory of paternalistic industrial relations was a prominent feature, however our analysis supports a view in which paternalism should not be seen as bounded by time but by social structure (Ackers, 1998). In this respect, the past has to be managed as well as the present. It is not necessarily the case that paternalism should be re-invigorated, but that its positive features can be drawn upon in certain contexts. The lock cases, while unique contexts in their own right, are also not some local peculiarity. Our analysis can therefore feed into more general questions regarding the impact of modernisation processes within established sites all over the world.

Notes

1 Sections of this chapter were published under Greene, A.M., Black, J. and Ackers, P. (2001), 'Lost Narratives? From paternalism to team working in a lock manufacturing firm', *Economic and Industrial Democracy*, Vol. 22: 2.

2 This internal recruitment process caused the company to be investigated by the Commission for Racial Inquiry in the mid-1970s, when it was found that these recruitment practices perpetuated an unrepresentative all-white workforce. All jobs are now advertised in job centres, although they are still also advertised internally on notice boards, and the importance of knowledge of lock manufacturing makes this change more formal than in reality.

3 LockCo Shop Steward's Committee Meeting, 19 July 1995.

4 Meeting with the LockCo convenor 13 November 1997.

Chapter Three

Gender and Family: Industrial Relations Beyond the Factory Gates[1]

> We did try an experiment with a guy ... he needed a job and the sex equality being bandied about these days a lot, so they tries him on [assembling] but he wasn't suitable ... he just wasn't dextrous enough ... they're small you know and you've got to keep these things in your hands. I don't know how they do it, but some of these women do and they're quite happy ... if they talk about shopping and things like that it might take their mind off it, where I think a guy, it would drive virtually crazy ... We've found him another job.. and he's proving quite good since he's moved (male toolroom worker at LockCo, 1983).

In this chapter we aim to inform the analysis of the experiences of workers through a lens which sees gender and wider family perspectives as central to an understanding of industrial relations. We connect with the themes drawn out in Chapter Two in recognising the importance of legacies of gendered social relations and gendered work, plus the influence of wider family structures and relationships on contemporary industrial relations experiences.

Gender and Family: a Conventional Account

There is a serious neglect of gender perspectives within conventional Western industrial relations accounts. As Wajcman recently argues:

> ... a glance at the contents of the mainstream journals and textbooks indicates that, although some progress has been made, gender issues remain marginal to much of the current research agenda (2000, p. 183).

Such neglect is criticised from two main viewpoints. The first involves the fact that conventionally, industrial relations research has focused predominantly on both manufacturing and male manual worker regimes (Rubery and Fagan, 1995). Such sectors are declining within developed world contexts, with growth areas built predominantly around service sector jobs and amongst those working 'nonstandard' hours (part-time, casual, temporary, self-employed), of which women are predominant. The decline of male manufacturing employment and the rise of feminised service work begins to ask different questions about the employment relationship which are currently not being dealt with (Wacjman, 2000; Ackers, 1999).

Secondly, even that literature which has focused exclusively on manufacturing research has not subjected the analysis to a gendered gaze (Sayce, forthcoming; Lawrence, 1996). Sayce (forthcoming) provides a useful summary of industrial relations studies, which have overlooked gender as an issue of analysis, despite significantly male or female workforces or gendered job demarcations. For example, Darlington's (1994) longitudinal study of Merseyside workplace unionism appears to ignore that at one of the plants the majority of the workforce was female and deserved comparison on this with the other two predominantly male workforces. Similarly, Delbridge's (1998) study of Welsh component factories, fails to discuss gender as important to industrial relations experiences despite the number of women workers. Within this, it should also be recognised that gender relates to men and women, however the significance of male-dominated contexts on the nature of industrial relations is usually neglected. This is even though studies such as Collinson (1994) indicate the impact of masculine identities on behaviour and relationships within workplace contexts.

The debate about the need to include gendered accounts of men's experiences is valid and indeed we should recognise that:

> ... a gender analysis of industrial relations is not simply about adding 'women's issues' to the list of research topics or noting the impact of industrial relations systems on women (Wacjman, 2000, p. 195).

However, we feel a focus on women within industrial relations is justified (Greene, forthcoming). In particular, given the interest within this volume, we need to look at what voices are being heard within mainstream industrial relations and which are not. The experiences of women workers and how these differ from those of male workers are left unanalysed in most industrial relations accounts. The problem is that if voiced accounts are not utilised, those without power resources are left unheard. As the experiences discussed within conventional industrial relations are male, there is a tendency to treat workers as homogenous, with this homogeneity based around male experience. Similarly, as Rubery and Fagan (1995) point out, where 'atypical' or 'nonstandard' workers are discussed, they too are discussed as a homogenous group with little understanding of the varieties of experience of part-time, casual or clerical workers (predominantly women), which their international comparative analysis has indicated. There is thus a need to 'make visible aspects of an employment and industrial relations systems that tend to remain hidden when analysts fail to interrogate the information with gender related issues in mind' (Rubery and Fagan, 1995, p. 212).

The Significance of Occupational Segregation by Gender

The neglect of gender issues within mainstream industrial relations is of concern as it is obvious that gender impacts upon work experience. Labour market research has long recognised the salience of analysis of gender, in particular involving issues of gendered segmentation of jobs and inequities of pay between men and women.

The gendered segmentation of jobs has been a significant issue within equality theorising and policy-making even if it has not formed part of the dominant industrial relations paradigm in the West. Hakim (1979; 1992) points to the obvious occupational segregation which exists in the British labour market. This includes both horizontal segregation (the separation of occupations into 'men's' and 'women's' jobs), and vertical segregation (where men typically work in higher grade occupations or posts and women are concentrated into lower level jobs, or where men are promoted higher up career ladders within occupations). There appears to have been little change over the last two decades. While there has been an overall decline in occupational sex segregation 1979–89, this conceals marked differences in the rates of integration of men and women across occupational groups (Watts and Rich, 1993; Anker, 1997). The main concern is that segregation declined relatively slowly in those areas where segregation is highest; namely, male dominated and female dominated occupations. While in 1979 over four-fifths of men were in occupations where they outnumbered women (half of men were in occupations where they outnumbered women nine to one), in 1990 the situation was little changed apart from the fact that there was a shrinking in the exclusively male occupations (Hakim, 1992). As Cockburn (1991) identifies, everyday observation shows occupations to be sharply segregated into male jobs and female jobs. Such segregation is not exclusive to Britain. Studies indicate the varying degrees of gendered occupational segregation across Europe (Kirton and Greene, 2000a) and worldwide (Anker, 1997).

The British Equal Opportunities Commission's position on occupational segregation is that it is inequitable because it places restrictions on people's freedom to choose the job that they do (Hakim, 1992). In essence, occupational segregation is a force for labour market rigidity and inefficiency; it is wasteful of human resources and a source of inflexibility within a context of globalisation, where flexibility is stressed (Anker, 1997). More importantly, it is particularly detrimental to some groups of workers, notably women, and thus has a negative effect on how they are viewed in the workplace and on their status and income. Occupational segregation is significant as it is generally agreed that particularly vertical segregation, is by far the most important explanation of the sex differential in earnings and women's weak position in the labour market generally (Treiman and Hartmann, 1981; OECD, 1988; Anker, 1997).

Hakim's (1991, 1995, 1992) research indicates significant support for a human capital explanation of occupational segregation by sex and is an attempt to challenge accounts which saw women as 'victims' of social structures and attitudes. The main proposition is that while women are disproportionately in the lowest status and lowest paid jobs, they are also disproportionately satisfied with their jobs. This is explained by the fact that the majority of women aimed for a 'homemaker' career and work is seen as of peripheral importance. Her findings indicated that only a minority of women, are committed to work as a central life goal. Hakim distinguished between two groups of women workers, those few who worked full time and had stronger work commitment, and the majority of part-time women workers who had lower levels of work commitment than men do. In other words, occupational segregation is not imposed upon women, it derived from women's work orientations and life priorities. Thus Hakim goes so far as to state; 'most women have actively colluded in their own imprisonment in unpaid work in the home and low-paid, low status jobs in the workforce' (1991, p. 110).

Hakim's thesis has been the subject of debate, particularly involving criticism of her view of the role of women in the labour market as rational economic agents, where the 'experience of women' regardless of social and historical context is generalised upon (Anker, 1997; Scheibl, 1996). This is also a criticism of many approaches to equality initiatives predicated on a philosophy of 'sameness'; that people should have access to and be assessed within the workplace as individuals, regardless of social category (for example gender) and we would add, irrespective of the particular context. Liberal equality initiatives, particularly those enshrined in law, are based on the individual, where people are required to deny or attempt to minimise differences, and compete solely on grounds of individual merit (Liff and Wajcman, 1996; Jewson and Mason, 1986). Within a free market philosophy, policies based on the neutral individual are seen as the most efficient means of achieving a fair distribution of resources in the workplace. Apart from extensive literature criticising such approaches for failing to deliver equality in the workplace or breakdown gendered segregation (see Webb, 1997; Liff, 1996; Cockburn, 1989), the issue of achieving equality is clearly more complex than this. Thus we agree with Judy Lown that:

> the constant reification of capitalism obscures the historical reality of both capitalists and workers as gendered beings with different interests and stakes in the material features of employment and marital arrangements (1986, p. 36).

The Significance of Family and Community

Other gender-related areas that have suffered neglect within conventional industrial relations include family and community. As Ackers ruefully comments, 'Industrial relations has lost sight of family, community and wider society altogether' (1999, p. 2). Thus, not only do conventional industrial relations studies retain a divide between home and work, public and private, but also, the salience of inter-relationships between work and family lives experienced by men *and* women is overlooked (Wacjman, 2000). Ackers provides a useful summary of industrial relations literature, citing how key industrial relations writers such as Hugh Clegg (1979) have absolutely no reference to the family, while more recent texts such as Edwards (1995) or Sisson (1994) continue to 'treat men and women as atomised economic actors, neglecting how they combine in families to support each other and their children' (Ackers, 1999, p. 4). New developments within employment such as flexible working, part-time working and decentralisation are dealt with as issues for management or governmental strategy, without recognising that family dynamics have impacted upon the expansion of part-time employment or more flexible working (Cockburn, 1991). As Ackers continues, the new industrial relations issues may revolve 'less around the internal workplace "frontiers of control" than the tension between working and family life- although the two are inter-related' (1999, p. 4).

In particular, a deep understanding and appreciation of the social and historical context in which industrial relations is played out is necessary to understand the success or failure of policies and to assess what men's and women's 'choices', interests and stakes, may be within particular situations. Gendered occupational segregation and kinship and community linkages, are obvious parts of the structure of work and of workplace relations within the two lock firms of our study, both before and after the restructuring process. Our contention is that the reactions to, and the impact of, the restructuring of traditional work organisation at the two lock firms, must be contextualised within an ethnographic account, in order to be understood. This allows gender dimensions to play a significant analytical role.

Gender and Family: an Ethnographic Account

What an ethnographic account (and particularly one which is based at shopfloor rather than managerial level) offers is a way of tapping into voices which are usually left unheard: notably of women. Indeed, while mainstream industrial relations research is criticised because of its neglect of gender and family, it is through ethnography that women as workers began to make an appearance within industrial relations. Thompson and Ackroyd (1999) point to the new generation of feminist industrial sociologists appearing in the early 1980s, notably Pollert (1981), Cavendish (1982) and Westwood (1984), all of whom, through ethnographic methods, were able to closely observe informal practices. Thus, distinctively female modes of action within workplace cultures began to emerge, reflecting the different forms of solidarity and sociability arising from interaction within wider family and community networks (Thompson and Ackroyd, 1999, p. 51).

With reference to the lock companies, a concern to capture the informal is significant as women's voices are easy to miss in the hierarchy of the lock companies as there is clear occupational segregation on the shopfloor within the two firms. The restructuring introduced by the new owners into both firms therefore had significant implications (both potential and realised) for equality issues within the factories. Experiencing the changes to work organisation first, it was KeyCo that provided the 'testing ground' with regard to the impact of restructuring on occupational gendered segregation for LockCo.

The shopfloor work organisation and employment structures at the two lock firms traditionally demonstrated clear occupational segregation of jobs based around gender. The amount of women working in the industry has declined somewhat since the early 1980s, indeed the visits to LockCo in 1983 and 1987 found around two-thirds of the workforce was female, while presently, women account for around 50 per cent at the two companies. Until the late 1980s at KeyCo and the late 1990s at LockCo, there was clear evidence of horizontal and vertical segregation (Hakim, 1979, 1992). Men held the skilled and semiskilled jobs; tool-making and tool-changing, polishing, dipping, engineering and maintenance work. Women were predominantly assemblers and packers, with some women holding positions in the warehouse and checking stock. As a response to the Equal Pay and Sex Discrimination legislation, the industry wages system was rationalised in 1974 into a more complex grading system formally ending the division between male and female jobs. However, 'semiskilled' women workers in practice were only graded from G to D, while 'skilled' men were graded from C to A. The formal grading thus came to closely mirror gender divisions on the shopfloor and by the late 1980s, had come to increasingly follow the distinction between semi/unskilled direct piece workers who were predominantly female and indirect workers who were predominantly male.

At KeyCo, the abolition of piecework, the introduction of cellular manufacturing and a move towards functional flexibility had significant effects on the gendered segmentation of work within the firms. The regrading of jobs that accompanied the restructuring, placed all employees, regardless of gender, within three grade bands. While the top grade was reserved for the most skilled work (predominantly male), the majority of employees were placed in grade one. This regrading also abolished the traditionally male position of foreman and the predominantly male charge hand position. To replace these positions, a team leader role at grade two was introduced and employees appointed after an application and assessment procedure. This saw a dramatic increase in the numbers of women in positions of responsibility at shopfloor level, than had originally held charge and positions. In addition, employees now worked in gender mixed teams, which were expected to be functionally flexible around a band of tasks, many of which crossed over what were traditionally gender-segregated jobs. Thus for example, men were expected to assemble and pack if necessary, and women were expected to tool change and carry out machine maintenance. Managers were aware of the segregation which existed; the Engineering Manager stated: 'Well … assemblers are female and they do as the men tell them to do is the general rule.'

The restructuring plans were seen as an emancipatory force for the workforce by both KeyCo managers and the KeyCo union convenor who felt that the changes would be positive, in terms of offering people more interesting jobs, and increasing control and autonomy. One of the line managers also commented on her experience as one of the first female supervisors in the factory: 'I think we [women managers] have got a lot of respect at all levels because it hasn't been easy to get where we've got in this environment.' The Personnel Director reflected on the overall strategy within the change process:

> we had to get away from the principle that 'this is my job, and I'm not letting anybody else do it', to 'this is my role in KeyCo, I've got to train other people on it and I've got to move over there and do her or his job as well' and the whole issue of flexibility and mobility of skills.

The female union convenor was particularly glad that the change process is attempting to break down the gender demarcations:

> yes we are [breaking down the traditional barriers], and it's lovely ... I thought we'd never get that but we have, we've even got some of the men ... they're getting into it and enjoying it, whereas others just set the machine and that's it, end of story.

However it is the response of workers to these changes and their effects on the segmentation of jobs which is the focus of this account.

Occupational Segmentation as Part of Contemporary Identity Construction

In the 1990s, the 'taken-for-granted' assumption that certain types of work were a male or female preserve was still deeply embedded on the shopfloor and was evident in the discourse of the workers at both firms. Given the extent to which large complex family networks still exist, kinship networks were key to the recruitment and retention of workers where an internal labour market very much depended on recruiting family members. Skill thus becomes something which is kin-defined, with the family possessing substantial resources within certain employment contexts (Grieco, 1987b, p. 41; 1996). This is a common feature of those industries which are community based, such as carpets (Ackers, 1988), crystal glass (Black and Neathey, 1989), or steel making (Grieco, 1987a). It is interesting to note that men, women and older children came to work together in lock companies as families, unlike within Lancashire coal and cotton for example where men usually worked in one industry and women in the other. However, once the family came to work together in the lock industry, they then divided into distinctive gender roles.

Male workers continue to rationalise this segregation today by notions of gender-differentiated physical abilities. For example, some stated that they did not have small enough fingers to deal with the intricacies of assembling a lock. One toolmaker at LockCo commented that while women were currently undertaking training for all sorts of jobs:

> somehow it never seems right ... that the females should be hammering and crashing away ... men couldn't have done the jobs that women do ... the dexterity of their fingers and their application to doing that job was much more quick and definite than I could ever have achieved.

When one man was asked if he had to assemble the locks that he made the components for, he seemed quite aghast and stated: '*We* don't assemble them, the girls assemble and spray them' [emphasis added in line with transcriptions].

What is often more interesting and significant is what is implicit and not said: that which does not form a part of the dominant discourse (Potter and Wetherell, 1987). Thus, when asked if people would like to change anything about their jobs, the issue of taking on a job customarily held by the other gender was never raised. There was no suggestion of a desire to end the gender segregation of jobs. There also appears to have been little change in attitudes since the early 1980s, as the quote at the beginning of this chapter indicates.

The embeddedness of the traditional segregation is also demonstrated in both the women's discourse and in some of their action. Most notably, this involved the difficulties faced by the companies and the union in attempting to persuade men and women to take on jobs formally seen as a gender preserve as part of the restructuring programmes. The union convenor at KeyCo specifically commented on the difficulty she faced in persuading women to take on 'male' roles. While as part of the new flexibility agreement and new grading structure, women were expected to take on tool changing and maintenance work, the women themselves were often sceptical that they were able to do it. As the convenor remarked:

> many have surprised themselves cause they were convinced cause they've been put into this slot all these years that they was just assemblers, nothing else. I had one woman who was convinced that she could never change the machine and the first time she was shown she said 'God is that all it is? Ain't it easy'.

The difficulty was getting past the stereotype of the women's image of themselves; their industrial identity, and persuading them to try. This very positive experience was also countered however by the attitudes of some women towards the changes, which the union convenor found particularly frustrating. The fact remains that while new mixed gender teams existed within KeyCo and LockCo after the restructuring, for the most part, women and men tended to have mobility *within* their gendered demarcations, rather than *across* gender boundaries. This reflects widespread criticism of the way in which flexibility initiatives do not deliver on the potential force they have for delivering greater gender equality (Dickens, 1997, p. 284). What the foregoing account has established clearly, is that women's and men's experiences of their work were significantly different: we could not talk about a homogenous workforce, in the way that many industrial relations studies assume.

Significantly, with regard to the women workers, we can also begin to further understand their attitudes towards gendered job demarcations. In particular, there was no contemporary experience of women challenging the occupational segregation which existed, or its detrimental effects. Notably, there was an absence of complaints from women about their pay levels. The union convenor related one example of a woman at KeyCo who had asked her, 'why should a woman earn that much money? It should only be men.' This was similar to viewpoints found at LockCo with regard to the relative fairness of the grading structure, reflecting a similar self-image. While the majority of those interviewed at LockCo were dissatisfied with their levels of pay and felt that the grading system is unfair, the only positive remarks came from women. Here, their comments indicated an overall acceptance of the skill differential, and the fact that a higher skilled job should mean a higher grade and therefore wages. Thus when one of the women was asked to expand on her viewpoint, she simply stated: 'if the job's a higher grade, well it just is.' Views had not changed that much over the period from 1983 either, indeed a third had positive views of the grading system, including a woman who stated:

> because a lot of jobs aren't skilled jobs, I mean the jobs on our section aren't skilled, as I say children could do them if they looked at them, but if it's a skilled job … the gradings are all right.

Women's dissatisfaction with pay levels focused around the need to make the timing of jobs fairer so that piece rates between women are more equitable; again concerns *within*, rather than *across* gender demarcations.

Struggles over pay had been a feature of the overall employee discourse since the early 1980s at LockCo, however this was characterised predominantly by complaints from within the male sections of the workforce. For example in the 1980s, concerning the way in which the changes to the grading structure of 1975 had reduced the differential between skilled tool room workers and semiskilled assemblers and machinists. By the late 1990s, even this dissatisfaction with the grading system had dissipated and dissatisfaction with the level of wages was expressed with regard to comparisons outside the factory and where the grading structure is teamed with a merit system. Again this was a concern only for those skilled male workers who are eligible for a merit rise. The inequality of pay between men and women was not expressed by those women who we spoke to.

Gendered Social Spaces on the Shopfloor

It became clear that occupational segregation had a deeper significance than purely economic consequences, in the same way, as we discussed in the previous chapter, that piecework had a wider social importance than just a form of payment. Indeed gender identities played a part in the construction of wider group identities and social contact on the shopfloor. In essence, like piecework, gendered work was a 'way of life' for the lock workers. The gender mix of workgroups was seen as an important factor in the sociability of work and both men and women had built up social networks within the workplace that were integral to their satisfaction with their work experience. Gender identity emerged as an important structuring element of shopfloor life. Men at LockCo commented on the extent to which working with a large group of men made work a more sociable activity than if they worked with women: 'It's all men ... which is acceptable to the majority of us ... we'd rather work with men, than sort of with men and women ... it's a good atmosphere.' Another added in a similar vein, that work is more sociable for him because: 'It's also the only all male place isn't it, except for the secretary, on the company like.' Equally, one woman commented that her work was not a social activity because: 'round by me, mainly it's men ... it's the locksmiths.' This gendered social aspect of work was an important part of their work experience. Exactly similar attitudes were also found at KeyCo, even after the restructuring which had broken down many of the physical gender boundaries within teams on the shopfloor. As one woman commented: 'we don't bother much with the men. But the girls are great ... we're like a family', while a man also recognised the gender division which still existed on the shopfloor: '... the girls tend to stick together and then there's us.' In other words, women and men were not taking advantage of the new emancipated 'genderless' shopfloor which management and the KeyCo union convenor enthusiastically proclaimed.

Other ethnographic studies, notably Roy (1960), indicate the importance of social contact as a significant part of coping with the experience of factory work. At the lock firms, this was gendered social contact. Like Roy's experience in the 'clicking room', one key source of job satisfaction at the lock companies lay in the informal interaction shared by members of the workgroup. In general, women's work on the shopfloor was monotonous and relentless. When LockCo workers were asked what level of control and autonomy they had over their own work, all of those who stated that they experienced a lack of control were women. In general, men had more control over the pace and organisation of their work. Not all of these women desired more control however, and those who did, would like to make their jobs easier. Others stated that they would like more control, but did not think there were the opportunities on the shopfloor, and were therefore more accepting of the situation: 'I don't think they'd let you would they?' This is mirrored by a comment from the other piece worker who had commented on the lack of control but who stated: 'I don't think you could on the shopfloor really.'

The overall impression of traditional 'women's work' was of the lack of skill, control and its repetitive nature. As one woman at LockCo commented: 'I mean you don't need your brains out there ... cause when you're working you're not really thinking about what you're doing.' This was recognised by the men too: '... mainly the production workers were female and I often used to wonder how they could stick it. Just doing that one operation year in year out you know.' The coping strategy for women was recognised as deriving from their social interaction with other women, as this man continued: 'but then apparently they can just switch off and think about the kid's schooling.' Indeed, this issue formed part of the justification of the segmentation of jobs on gender grounds with another aspect of the men's inability to do 'women's jobs' being due to the fact that:

> I don't know how they do it, but some of these women do, and they're quite happy ... if they talk about shopping and things like that, it might take their mind off it, where I think a guy, it would drive virtually crazy.

This has resonance with the experience of shopfloor women in Pollert's (1981) ethnographic study in the tobacco industry, where women accept that their jobs would be too boring for the men to cope with. In a similar way to the lock workers, the women in the tobacco firm relate the way in which they continue their jobs with robotic dexterity, while they stimulate their minds with conversations with their work mates (usually concentrated on what might be characterised as 'women's issues' of marriage, sex, children, abortion). Thus the experience of the women lock workers reflects the:

> cutting off or separating the 'inner self' from what is objectively happening on the 'outside' [which is] one of the sorry 'skills' we are forced into, in an existence dominated by alienated relations of production (Pollert, 1981, p. 131).

Women's attitudes towards opposing a breakdown of the gendered division of labour may be partly explained in terms of the notion of gendered social space. The convenor at KeyCo was frustrated that many women did not react positively to the restructuring process and embrace their new 'empowered' job roles. However, studies in other organisational contexts suggest that within gendered demarcations, women can positively develop spaces for themselves within otherwise male dominated spaces. Within office work, talking about families and domestic life, gossiping and personalising conversations become forms of resistance which are distinctively feminine (Barker and Downing, 1980, p. 82). On the one hand, this domestic stereotype of women's social space in the lock factories was used as a justification for the maintenance of unequally rewarded gendered demarcated jobs. However, while they were researching within a white collar and predominantly female work context, Barker and Downing's findings have resonance with the experience of the women in the lock factories:

> the significance of the culture we have attempted to describe ... is indeed a factor in the reproduction of women's oppression, but it can also be seen as the development of an informal work culture which cannot be penetrated by 'masculine' work standards (ibid., p. 83).

Similarly, Pollert (1981, p. 130) identifies the informal shopfloor culture that is created by women and notes the strength of the female groups, compared to the mixed groups or where the worker is left to work individually. In a similar vein to Barker and Downing, Pollert notes that the women 'mucking in' for a laugh, could lead to collusion in shopfloor sexism, but that within this: 'sexual oppression at work also has its own dynamic. It provokes resistance – both to patriarchy and to the work discipline often mediated by it' (ibid., p. 234). Men dominate the decision-making processes within the lock industry and have both higher status and pay than women. However there were traditional female spaces on the shopfloor which excluded the men, where men did not feel comfortable working. Such female spaces were threatened by the restructuring at KeyCo. Therefore, in-depth voiced accounts have offered further explanations for the ostensible failure of the restructuring programme, building on the discussion in the last chapter.

Historical Occupational Segmentation at the Lock Firms

In line with the emphasis within the last chapter, it is also important to recognise the historical legacy of gendered nature of lock work. The long history of the lock industry adds another level of embeddedness of gendered jobs. It is not just that the gendered segmentation of jobs and inequalities in pay in the lock industry were a twentieth century phenomenon. Such gendered segmentation reflected long-standing traditions in existence since the early development of the industry. The gendered nature of skill categories has often been offered as an explanation for the way in which women have been assigned a subordinate position within the hierarchy of waged labour. Phillips and Taylor (1986, p. 55) argue that women's subordinate position derives from the negotiation and renegotiation of the labelling of skilled work and attempts by male workers to preserve their own skilled status at the expense of female workers. A similar discussion is found within the white-collar context of secretarial and office work context in Barker and Downing (1980). Thus, 'the sexualisation of skill labels following the actual deskil-ling of work processes ... is one which has been repeated throughout the course of the nineteenth and twentieth centuries' (Phillips and Taylor, 1986, p. 63).

However Pat Green extends this argument specifically within the lock industry, emphasising the need for a contextualisation of this discussion. Thus, 'women who worked in the 18th, 19th and the 20th centuries have by no means a certain route imposed upon them by virtue of the Industrial Revolution' (Green, 1989, p. 4). The deskilling model is inadequate when dealing with a diversity of trades and industries. Thus, within the lock industry, mass customisation did not automatically lead to the deskilling, negotiation of skill and subsequent subordination of women within the industry. When they did enter the labour market, it was already within distinctively different kinds of jobs; the labour market was already segmented. This was a distinctive feature of the lock industry as Green's (ibid., p. 8) historical investigation illustrates. While in other West Midlands metal industries (such as light chain, button and screw making), up to 90 per cent of the workforce were women, the number of women in the lock industry was only 10 per cent well into the 1860s. While apprenticeships were common for both boys and girls up to the mid-nineteenth century in other industries, there is no evidence of girls being apprenticed to the lock trade. Men were the locksmiths, and women were lock-workers. While these categories of work had become less stringent, demarcations along gender lines remained.

Extension of the Domestic Structure to the Workplace

The ethnographic account also directs us to the importance of family and wider lock community in the experience of work. The traditional male domination of the lock industry in comparison to other Black Country trades was somewhat unusual and partly reflects the fact that other trades, for example, chain-making, were reliant on outworking, which would account for the predominance of women. However, this does not offer explanations for why the lock industry should necessarily be different. One suggestion is that this reflected a different social organisation of the family within the Willenhall area. A Parliamentary Report of 1843 indicates some differences in the family and social conditions of families within the West Midlands. In comparison to other areas in the county, Willenhall was noted for the domestic accomplishments of its girls and women who: 'can do needlework, knit, cook and mend or make clothes, which may truly be regarded as extraordinary accomplishments among girls of the working classes' (Green, 1989, p. 12). Such wide differences within domestic conditions across small geographic distances are also reflected in Roberts' (1996) description of family life and women's experiences between three towns in Lancashire 1890–1940. Further research would be needed to establish whether this distinctive domestic organisation was a result of, or cause of, the development of segmented roles within the lock industry. What is certain is that family organisation can have a significant influence on the roles played by each sex within waged labour. Thus the family represents:

> particular constellations of ideals and values [where] relations of male supremacy are located in the sauce-cultural significance of familial relations as an organising principle of society (Lown, 1986, p. 30).

Through both oral and written life histories, Roberts (1996) identifies the way in which working class women in Lancashire at the turn of the twentieth century did appear to have a different work orientation to men, where women worked until they were married, with their ultimate aim being to leave work and set up home. Certainly, at the similarly craft oriented and paternalistic firm to the lock companies, of the Courtaulds silk mill, Lown finds how women's work patterns were related to their child bearing cycle, where the socialised values of family life were used as an organising principle of workplace relations (1983, p. 35). Such detailed information is not available for the lock industry, however, in a similar way to the experience of Courtaulds, there is evidence in the early to mid-1900s of employer, union and male worker opposition to women's employment, where a number of strategies were aimed at reducing the number of married women working. Minutes of the lock union of 1922 indicate that the Joint Industrial Council (JIC) should suggest that married women should not be employed, while in 1933 the Willenhall district committee requested that the JIC explicitly state what women's physical capacity would allow them to do, so that they would not be demeaning themselves doing men's jobs within the factories (Stenner, 1989, pp. 46, 77). In 1935, in response to the employer's argument that they needed to employ more women to meet foreign competition, the Lockunion's General Secretary stated 'so far as foreign competition was concerned they had never said they would not try to beat them, but they would never be a party to saying that our people should live like the foreigners' (ibid., p. 81). Thus a discourse was utilised whereby the idea of women doing male lock work were negatively characterised as the 'other' or 'foreign'.

We also need to link to the discussion in the previous chapter. The existence of paternalism as a traditional management style (Greene et al., 2000) may also provide some overarching explanation for the gendered roles. As Lown (1983) identifies, the concept of paternalism links to family values and therefore systems of patriarchal authority. Paternalism 'relies heavily on an appeal to personal ties of dependency and that these ties are interpreted in familial terms' (ibid., p. 34). It thus becomes a way in which patriarchal authority can be legitimated through social interaction. The notion of paternalism is at its root patriarchal, ingrained with connotations of mature, male authority (Kerfoot and Knights, 1994). Referring back to the *Encyclopaedia of the Social Sciences*, the definition of paternalism involves 'a type of behaviour by a superior toward an inferior resembling that of a male parent to his ... son' (Bennett, 1968). In addition, the previous chapter has also supported a new direction for accounts of paternalism within industrial relations. This involves eschewing narrow, economistic explanations of working class attitudes, and recognising how they need to be widened by looking at the way in which notions of paternalism, and worker support for paternalistic structures draw on 'the wider circles of community [and] family' (Ackers, 1998, p. 178).

Differences in technological developments are also important, particularly in reinforcing the influence of family structure on the organisation of the industry. As evidence indicates but conventional industrial relations has neglected: 'Gender is shown time and time again to be an important factor in shaping the organisation of work that results from technological change' (Wacjman, 2000, p. 190). Mass customisation of the lock industry through technological advancement did not come until the early to mid-twentieth century. This was significant in perpetuating the proliferation of small workshops well into the early 1900s; indeed there were still 30 in Willenhall

Portraits of a lock factory over time

Plate 1 The LockCo Factory and Lock Workers 1982: a Year before the Research Project Began (source: Hedges and Beynon, 1982)

Plate 2 The LockCo Factory 2000. The Changed Brand Names Reflect the Takeovers

The significance of the lock industry to the town of Willenhall

Plate 3 Model of a Key, Willenhall High Street, 2000

Plate 4 The Lock Museum, Willenhall High Street, 2000

in the late 1980s (Green, 1989, p. 13) and the union convenor talked about hand polishing of locks being carried out in a number of household workshops even in the late 1990s. While conditions have doubtlessly changed, historical accounts of these small family workshops in the early 1900s document the gendered work roles and how these were integrated with child rearing and wider family and domestic life: 'every little house got a place ... they would have a vice, a woman would have a child strapped to her back and would be doing the filing' (Stenner, 1989, p. 46) The skilled locksmith, however, still maintained an integral part within the lock-making process. While mass production was certainly accompanied by increasing numbers of women into the industry over the 1940s and 1950s (Stenner, 1989), the skilled locksmith was and is still necessary today to service a number of custom made locks within the lock companies.

The point of this historical discussion is to illustrate that women carried out separate tasks from the male locksmiths right from the early development of the industry. Women's experiences in the lock trade covered the period from the earliest development, but even within the small family workshops, their work was qualitatively different to that of the men's, involving filing, lacquering and packing, while the 'handmade' element remained in the hands of the individual male locksmith (Green, 1989, p. 14). The evidence suggests that at no time did women step into the male skilled role, not even at a time of labour shortage and urgent need for increased production such as during the world wars (ibid., p. 17). Men within the lock industry therefore did not appear to have been under serious threat of their skill status being reduced or diluted by the introduction of women. Thus, referring back to Phillips and Taylor (1986), there is some evidence to suggest that men and women within the lock industry were never in a position to negotiate or renegotiate their skill labels; they experienced significantly separated work tasks from the start. This firstly indicates the importance of contextualised accounts to explore the utility of macro-theorising. Secondly, in specific reference to the lock industry, such analysis indicates the historical embeddedness of the separation of tasks, thus highlighting how much of a break with tradition, were the new restructuring policies at the lock companies.

Towards a Gendered Ethnographical Account of the Restructuring Process

Conventional industrial relations analysis, particularly that which is conducted within a quantitative paradigm, would no doubt have indicated the ostensible failure of the change process to dramatically alter the pattern of working on the shopfloor. Additionally, such analysis would probably have indicated the opposition to the breakdown of gendered jobs by those who are seen to benefit most from change, the women lock workers. However, the analysis needs to be situated within the wider historical context and needs to hear the voices of those women and men involved to attempt to understand the situation. It is important to understand the contextualised nature of the gendered segmentation of work, within the historical and sociological traditions of the specific firm, industry and community. In particular, the foregoing analysis, drawn from the discourse of the workers involved, plus oral and documentary life histories, indicates that in terms of gendered work within the lock industry, behaviour, relations and structures were framed and scripted in a particularly gendered way. This related to embedded 'ways of doing things' over many generations, as well as reflecting the family and community nature of lock working: a particular drama of gender relations. The new management's mistake was in not recognising this particular drama of the employment relationship, in much the same way as the drama of paternalism (discussed in Chapter Two) was ignored.

This points to the dangers of equality strategies, which are often implemented in a context-blind way. Resistance by the women workers at the lock companies, to what was seen by management and union officials as liberating and emancipatory change, was bound up with gendered occupational identities. A change in the gendered nature of jobs thus posed a threat to many women's and men's occupational identities. It also threatened the social group formation and identities on the shopfloor, which the discourse of the workers suggested was organised around gender lines. Attempts to end the gender divided segregation of jobs are presented as positive and emancipatory. However, such a view often neglects two significant factors. Firstly it neglects the strength of this segregation in the construction of identities (Cockburn, 1991; Beechey, 1980; Hartmann, 1979; Burawoy, 1979). Therefore, to say that women 'collude in their own oppression' (Hakim, 1991) has limited explanatory value. In essence, whatever group of workers we are looking at, it must be acknowledged that choices and life goals are defined by the opportunity structures that exist in each context. Choice is socially constructed (Berger and Luckman, 1979) and constrained within the limits set by socially derived rules and expectations. The second factor is that gendered divisions can paradoxically, be a positive force, particularly for the women involved. It enables them to carve out space within a male dominated context (Pollert, 1981; Barker and Downing, 1980; Collinson and Collinson, 1989). Within the newly restructured lock companies, women's social interaction and female work identity may be threatened, as men are encouraged to encroach upon their jobs and social spaces and vice versa. This is not to play down the obvious detrimental effects of the gendered segregation of jobs, particularly on pay levels and status. However, ethnographic enquiry serves to illustrate the complexity of identities on the shopfloor and the contradictory and paradoxical situations that may arise from this complexity (Collinson, 1994, p. 52). It also reiterates the points made in the last chapter, emphasising the need for management and trade union representatives to be sensitive to, and to recognise the legitimacy and embeddedness of, traditional demarcations, if management are to have success in introducing changes to working practices.

The Relevance of Gender and Family to Developing World Industrial Relations

One needs to be careful not to draw artificial distinctions between agricultural and non-agricultural work in much of the developing world, particularly as many women are involved in both arenas, sometimes in combination and sometimes at different points in their life cycles (Grijns et al., 1994; Grieco et al., 1996). However, there seems to be a shared consensus by writers in the field that the integration of developing countries into the capitalist world economy has led to an overall deterioration in the chances and modes of survival for women (Mies, 1988). Early efforts by developing countries to industrialise have tended to follow the model of the West, which have predominantly had a negative impact on rural industries, many of which involved huge numbers of women workers (Grijns et al., 1994).

We identify interesting discussions relevant to gendered industrial relations analysis in the developing world context. Margaret Grieco (1996) and Judy Lown (1983) both point to the parallels between their historical discussions of occupational communities in the developed world, and their analysis of communities and industrial development in the developing world. As Lown (1983, p. 44) states:

> With the increasing penetration of capital into former agricultural economies all over the world, the need to analyse the interconnections between changes in household and kin organisation and production have been accentuated. The distance in time and geography between nineteenth-century Essex and twentieth-century countries of the Third World may seem gigantic but the conceptual equipment needed to make sense of the gender and class relationships in both may be much more similar than we sometimes allow ourselves to think.

In particular, it should be of no surprise that worldwide, women face considerable disadvantages compared to male workers. Such disadvantages mirror those in the developed world, namely, low-skilled and de-skilled work, atypical contracts (part-time, casual, temporary, self-employed), lower wages, lower training opportunities and the primary load of unpaid domestic labour in the family and at home (Grijns et al., 1994, ch. 3). Gendered occupational segregation is also a worldwide phenomena (Anker, 1997). Looking at the more micro-level, Grieco et al. (1996) provide detailed analysis of the gendered differentiation of jobs and skills within portering jobs in the urban context of Accra, Ghana. This not only defines what women and girls, boys and men could do, but also what technology they could use (women were headload carriers, men could use trolleys and carts) and subsequently the nature of the work and what they could expect to achieve in the way of payment.

As in the developed world, there is a wider societal view of women as temporary workers and secondary earners within the household, which affords them a lower status position than of men (Grace, 1990). Within this paradigm, a view of the male-led household is upheld, where female waged work is seen as a secondary contribution to the household economy. In addition, Third World women are commonly portrayed as having additional cultural attributes of docility, obedience and passivity, which makes women more attractive workers to employers; being cheaper, whilst also supporting and upholding their own subordination and oppression. Within industrial relations literature therefore, women in the developing world have been portrayed predominantly as victims of capitalism or as part of a puppetlike reserve labour force (Wolf, 1992). However, we should be careful also of assuming that women are an homogenous category, indeed, mirroring Wacjman (2000), cited earlier in this chapter, White criticises researchers in the developing world:

> ... the literature takes women as its category of analysis, attributes to it a homogeneity predicated on a basic sameness of oppression, and confuses its own construction of the category with an actually existing and coherent group of women sharing similar interests (1992, p. 158).

This then means that differences amongst women are not identified, for example, key concepts such as marriage or the sexual division of labour are applied arbitrarily, rather than exploring their local meanings (Mohanty, 1984 cited in White, 1992). Ethnography obviously offers a methodology to attempt to explore these local meanings, so that White found a variety of practices and attitudes around what appeared at first to be similar cultural mores within the family contexts in Kumirpur.

Women do not hold positions of formal power within workplace contexts in the developing world, in much the same way that women do not in the developed world. This has often meant that women have been missing from accounts of waged work in much the same way as the Western paradigm of industrial relations has been criticised. This gap is significant because even research at the most superficial level, indicates that many of the gender stereotypes applied to the developing world are not lived out in experience. Many studies have indicated the incidence of female-led households, and where female waged income, rather than only secondary, is vital for the economic survival of the household in a wide variety of developing world settings. For example in Ghana, estimates indicate that around 60 per cent of urban households depend solely on women's income for family survival (Grieco et al., 1996, p. 9). Similar conclusions are drawn in Malaysia (Grace, 1990), Bangladesh (Kramsjo and Wood, 1992), India (Kasturi et al., 1990), and Indonesia (Grijns et al., 1994). Anyone following the international news during the 'Grand Labour Offensive' in South Korea of 1987–88 cannot have failed to notice that it was women textile workers who led the militant strike action and who suffered brutally at the hands of the male police force and state authorities (Bello and Rosenfeld, 1990). Further challenges to the image of the docile and passive Asian woman worker is evidence of organised solidarity groups such as SEWA (Self Employed Women's Association) in India (Kasturi et al., 1990) or the Proshika organisations in Bangladesh (Kramsjo and Wood, 1992), cursory statistical analysis of which, will demonstrate that 50 per cent of them are solely organised by women.

However, despite facts that provide challenges to the stereotypical view of gender relations within waged work in the developing world, such complexities of industrial relations have not reached conventional or mainstream accounts. A primary concern here is that women's voices are missing, as Wolf states:

> In many studies of third world women and industrial capitalism, the women themselves are missing, rendered undifferentiated, homogenous, faceless and voiceless (1992, p. 9).

For example, Grace's (1990) account of unionising women workers in the electronic industry in Malaysia is useful in highlighting the gender issues which are often missed in conventional analyses. However it suffers from being written solely from the perspective of the author: there are no voiced accounts to support and authenticate her account. Saito et al.'s (1982) study of women textile workers in Japan and Thailand is based on an impressively large questionnaire survey, plus interviews and observation. However again, the reader is presented with masses of statistics, analysed from the point of view of the authors, and with none of the richness of detail, which might have come from the observations or interviews. We do not begin to understand what it is like to be a woman worker and how this might differ from that of male workers.

It is here that ethnographic methods have much to offer. However, it should be noted that ethnographic accounts can also suffer from gender invisibility. We have already discussed the lack of gender perspectives to infuse Delbridge's (1998) or Darlington's (1994) account. Moving to a developing world context, while Ramaswamy's (1996) account of the rayon spinners in Delhi is a good example of an ethnographic industrial relations study, it should be noted that gender relations do not feature at all in the account. This is despite the fact that an all-male workplace will doubtlessly have interesting gender dimensions to be explored. Like conventional accounts in the developed world, even Ramaswamy's account remains planted firmly within the workplace. However, not only does this ignore the implications of an all male context, it also does not recognise the importance of wider family and community influences on work. Indeed, there is no discussion of the fact that these male workers have lives outside of the factory, which impact upon and are influenced by, the family, household and community context outside of the workplace. Some of the accounts discussed below offer alternative ways of studying industrial relations within developing world contexts.

Moving the Debate Forward: Authentic Voices, Authentic Accounts (II)

Diane Lauren Wolf's (1992) ethnographic account of rural women in Java taking up factory work includes women's voices from the beginning: her first chapter opens with the story of Rini, a factory daughter. Wolf's study extends over a five year period, includes survey data, she lived in a rural village for 12 months, visited 12 factories, lived in a women's factory dormitory for a month, used diaries kept by some of the women workers, kept observation notes, and interviewed a large number of the women workers, both within their workplace contexts and within their family households. Wolf's reflexive account of her research process is illuminating. She had originally intended on basing her study on the mass of quantitative data collected in an early visit. However, she had found that she needed to go back and spend an extended period of time collecting stories and observation from both daughters and parents in their family and work contexts, in order to begin to try and understand the social processes that existed. In essence, an account without voices was seen as of limited use in facilitating analysis and understanding.

Family and Kinship

Some of the links which we were beginning to uncover between work, family and community in the lock contexts, but which are often ignored in conventional industrial relations, are also clear in the stories of the Javanese women factory workers. Wolf found challenged, some of her own Western presumptions about factory life for rural women in Java. For instance, rural migration to factory work is often seen as necessary to the survival of the rural family. However, the women Wolf talked with are able to contribute little from their meagre salaries to the family economy. There are however also questions about whether factory life emancipates women from family patriarchy relations. The ethnographic account allows a view to emerge, which finds factory life to have a contradictory impact on the Javanese women involved. While they have more freedom of action than when they remained within the rural family setting, which largely derives from having an independent flow of income, familial patriarchy was often replaced by factory patriarchy, which constrains action in other ways. In addition, kinship systems are seen as having a great impact on the boundaries of the women's actions, behaviour and decisions, in the same way as we began to uncover in the lock companies. While the young girls often feel that taking up factory work is a bid for a sense of freedom, most stopped factory work when they married and returned to their villages and extended families.

Looking at factory workers in India, Kasturi et al. (1990) also find that the women she spoke to and observed had similar experiences of migrating to factory work. While industrialisation in the developing world is often seen as leading to the breakdown of the family as the central productive unit, Kasturi finds that core values were maintained in the caste and kinship clusters which formed in the new urban settings amongst the rural migrants.

Kinship and family are also seen as important influences on social relations within the workplace context in Kapferer's (1972) ethnographic study of a textile factory in Africa. He makes clear links between the social behaviour of the shopfloor and broader processes outside. For example, looking at occupational histories, Kapferer is able to offer insights into why people choose a 'family' career: in other words, jobs which members of the same family have participated in for generations. In both Chilwa's and Lyashi's story, kinship ties are important determinants of the job chosen or not chosen so that an extended internal labour market (Manwaring, 1984) draws in migrant labour on the basis of family connections. Such links are seen as important social 'currency' in the social transactions and interactions on the shopfloor, which form the core of Kapferer's analysis; affecting for example, mobilisation of industrial action (which is discussed in greater detail in Chapter Four of this volume).

Grieco et al. (1996) highlight similar experiences with regard to female headload carriers in Accra, Ghana. Here, the experience of the young girl porters, the *kayayoos*, is detailed, with many of them being drawn to certain parts of the city through family connections, and residing in accommodation based around loose kinship ties. *At Christmas and On Rainy Days* goes further then this however, providing a detailed, voiced analysis of the variety of female experiences of work, from the girl-child *kayayoo*, and the headload carrier transporting heavy loads with an infant strapped to her back, through to the elderly woman trading goods from her doorstep. Grieco et al. (1996, ch. 9) bring such stories alive with a whole chapter devoted to biographies of the whole spectrum of female traders, young to old. Such analysis reminds us that we are often in danger of treating female (or male) workers as a homogenous group also, when in fact, as Rubery and Fagan (1996) would concur, there is a large variety of family experiences of work to be considered. What is common to all however, is the wider influence of kinship and family networks on work 'choices': whether that be the impact of extended and fluid household boundaries more common to Ghana, or the choices made by a single mother working part-time in inner-city Britain.

Voiced research allows challenges to be made to assertions that close-knit communities need close physical proximity within theorising around social capital (Coleman, 1988, 1990; Putnam, 1993, 1995, 1998). Kinship and family ties can remain strong and directional over large distances as such migration studies indicate. Margaret Grieco (1996; 1987a), in studying the seasonal migration of hop workers of East London or the migration of steel workers from Corby develops theorising around collective skill built up within, and sustained by, family and kinship linkages. In a similar way, the lock workers' experience and expectations of work had been developed as part of embedded collective family and community memories.

Grieco et al. (1996) provide an overview of the variety of different experiences of work through a woman's life cycle. One element which is core to this account is that of children's participation in the labour markets of many developing world countries. Child labour is obviously not an issue in the developed world to the extent that it is in the developing. For instance, while historical accounts of the British lock industry indicate that children *were* certainly employed in family workshops in the nineteenth century (Green, 1989), in the developing world, child labour *is* still a very current problem. Kulshereshtha (1996) points to around 25,000 child labourers in the lock industry in India, while Grieco et al., 1996 provide voiced accounts of the boy and girl child porters working in Ghana. However, while the response of development agencies, and therefore of the developed world, has tended to be based around outlawing child labour, more sensitive accounts which look in detail at the context in which children are working (Grieco et al., 1996; Grootaert and Kanbur, 1995; Rodgers and Standing, 1981; Chandrasekhar, 1997) point to the limited success of such legislative strategies. Indeed Grieco et al. (1996, pp. 59–61) emphasise the counterproductive effects of outlawing child labour as children and their parents then become forced to pay large bribes to officials to allow their children to keep working undetected, and which casts the children as criminals.

We need to be more culturally aware so that we recognise the context in which certain practices and processes exist and try to understand the social interactions and transactions that accompany them. Legislating against child labour therefore is likely to only foster opposition and to intensify the burden on the children involved, in much the same way that the culturally unaware wholesale restructuring at the lock companies was bound to elicit the opposition that it did. What an ethnographic approach offers to the analysis is contextualised views, which recognise the importance of children's income from waged work to family survival and which direct us to find much more sensitive strategies for trying to sustain children's education and avoid their exploitation. For example, Grieco et al. (1996) believe that action to arrange schooling around the hours that the children work is a more practical suggestion. This would reduce the inevitable drop-out rate from schools and would give the children the education, social capital and aspirations that they need, in order to invest in their education and training for better jobs, without increasing the family burden.

Challenging the Stereotypes

We discussed earlier how even cursory analysis allows us to challenge the stereotypical view of the docile and obedient developing world woman worker. Within Kramsjo and Wood's (1990) analysis of the Proshika self-help organisations in Bangladesh we find over half of the organisations are run and participated in by women. Women are making all kinds of successful demands on land owners, village elders, employers and government officials: from fighting for rights to community ponds and housing land, challenging marriage and divorce customs, organising training sessions and courses to improve literacy, through to resisting exploitation by the rich by collective legal suits. Within these accounts however, we can hear the women themselves, rather than the views of the outside observer. As readers, we engage with quoted verbatim speeches at rallies, and detailed interviews with campaigners and their families.

In a similar way, Margold's (1999) account of women's struggles for political voice, challenges the compliant image of the female Filapina factory worker. The complexities of past and present expectations and experiences and links between family and work are drawn out in the voiced account, as we experience the ambiguities of Erlinda's viewpoints and try to understand her collective spirit: where it has come from and how it will affect her behaviour.

Such accounts offer us a much more powerful and authentic account than would a traditional industrial relations case study. Elizabeth Grace (1990) looks at unionisation of women electronic workers in Malaysia, and particularly at the role of the state. She is no doubt correct that 'virtually all-existing studies of unions in general in Malaysia ... have overlooked the role of gender in shaping the behaviour of the government' (ibid., p. 15). However, how much more convincing would have been her analysis of the important impact that the women workers had on government action, if we had been able to hear the voices of the women involved, rather than just an account from the view of the author.

Voiced accounts allow direct challenges to the conventional accounts of developing world industrial relations. As in the lock ethnographies, where we see how gendered demarcations are actually supported by women and men, because of the social identities which are bound up with gendered spaces on the shopfloor. By capturing the informal, the habitually unvoiced, we can also capture exceptions and differences. For example, Sarah White's (1992) *Arguing with the Crocodile* explores the militancy of Bangladeshi women in opposition to forces of exploitation, finding arenas of power for women where none is usually assumed by Western analysts. Her ethnographic study indicates that at least publicly women do bow to the dominant culture which defines and constrains their movements and activities, including the type of work they can undertake. However, these women also pursue strategies of resistance through secrecy, humour and stinging irony (1992, p. 137). As is the case in many of the accounts discussed in this chapter, we also begin to recognise the contradictory processes at work for women in employment. For example, how kinship and family ties continue to have important influences on work experiences. Or how traditions and established 'ways of doing things' remain contemporary, due to embedded collective memory associated with wider family and community ties. We begin to have a greater understanding of the constraints and opportunities that these conventionally held 'external' influences have on experiences at the workplace.

We can also begin to challenge stereotypes about what are considered to be appropriate subjects for study within industrial relations. In the lock ethnographies, we illustrated how social interaction and gendered social spaces provided women with considerable power within their workplace context. To perhaps a greater extent in many developing world contexts, cultural and religious mores mean that women often lack physical assets, which may afford them formal power. However, White finds that the sources of women's power are often found in informal social interactions and relationships, in essence, their social capital:

> The strong structural discouragement to female independence thus fosters women's concentration on their networks and relationships for social capital and these come to represent the crucial locus of female power (ibid., 93).

What is clear is that such loci of power, within social capital, would not be identified within the formal record: ethnographic inquiry is essential for identifying these informal resources.

Summary: Moving beyond Binarism

Studies in the developing world, perhaps because of the still predominantly rural or early urban context of waged labour, generally have paid more attention to the link between community, family and workplace processes and relations, so that industrial relations in the developed world may draw useful examples from the developing world studies. Kapferer comments similarly on:

> ... the contrary development of industrial sociology in Africa ... where explanations for work factors have been found in areas outside of the work context, for example customs, community and social processes originating outside of work factors ... unlike Western sociology, which is severely criticised for explaining work behaviour solely in terms of social organisation of the work context (1972, p. 2).

For example, one can draw immediate parallels between the image of women lock workers filing with babies on their backs in the small family workshops of the 1900s with similar images of women porters in Accra (Grieco et al., 1996). The development of segregated occupational roles as a consequence of the 'fit' between new technologies (be this heavy tooling machinery in the lock industry at the turn of the century, or the use of bicycles and trolleys in portering) and child care responsibilities, would be an interesting 'take' on the development of skill and skill categories within the processes of the industrial revolution and a useful angle for future research.

With regard to ideas of embedded collective memory, we can begin to make links between the findings of the last two chapters. Chapter Two highlighted the importance of recognising historical legacy and embedded experience to contemporary industrial relations: particular dramas of management-labour relations were expected. Chapter Three has added gender and family dimensions to these dramas, so that for example, gendered segmentation in the past, is seen as very important as a structuring principle of contemporary industrial relations. This last point indicates how industrial relations ethnographies can move the theorising forward, regarding links between developing and developed world contexts. We can certainly draw parallels between the nineteenth century women lock workers, and women headload carriers in Ghana, or the historical accounts of kinship organisation of women's work in Lown's Courtauld silk mill and that of Javanese women textile workers.

However, the contemporary voiced accounts go further and *should* go further than just comparing historical developed contexts with contemporary developing contexts. Such a view only supports the conventional binarism between developing and developed, traditional and modern, which we find to be limiting. The lock ethnographies demonstrate how important are gendered family and community structures, which have a long historical legacy to contemporary relations and experiences. The few voiced accounts of industrial relations which we find in the developing world (largely within anthropological arenas) demonstrate the importance of links between family, household, gender and workplace relations, which we find in few developed world industrial relations studies excepting the lock ethnographies or more historical accounts. We need to consciously reverse the notion that advanced industrial societies always provide lessons for the less industrial (Curtis, cited in Marsden, 1994, p. 56). Thus, while accounts in the developed world tend to see labour migration as occurring rural to urban and labour circulation (rural to urban to rural in a cycle) as primarily a Third World phenomena, Grieco (1996) shows clearly that labour circulation formed part of working experience within the developed world amongst the London hop workers.

Therefore, we can use such a discussion as a way of moving the study of industrial relations forward, there should be continuous cross currents between developed and developing world contexts, with much to be learnt on both sides. In essence, we should be aiming to gain a more sensitive comparative approach: '… looking not to classify societies as more or less unequal … but to discover how and why differentiation takes place' (White, 1992, p. 161).

Note

1 Sections of this chapter are published under Greene, A.M., Ackers, P. and Black, J. (forthcoming), 'Going Against the Historical Grain: Perspectives on gendered occupational identity and resistance to the break down of occupational segregation in two manufacturing firms', in a special issue on power, representation and voice in *Gender, Work and Organisation*.

Chapter Four

Collective Action: Industrial Relations and the Mobilisation of Solidarity[1]

> A lot of my role and interaction is theatre ... Image is all important [management] is testimony to that, they say a lot but mean very little, it's all about rhetoric, presentation. The TUC school of thought says you have to tell the truth and that is right, but the way you present that truth is important, you have to present it in a way that will yield confidence (LockCo Trade Union Convenor).

In the last two chapters, we have outlined how important is a context of embedded experiences and attitudes to the nature of workplace industrial relations. From the workers at the lock companies, there was an overall feeling of negativity towards management, however, this stood alongside a desire for cooperation within the employment relationship, and an underlying loyalty and a positive view of working in the lock industry. However, the discourse of workers also suggested that people have a view of the limits of this cooperation, especially with regard to relations between union and management. Here, we would like to introduce a third 'drama of the employment relationship', outlining the ways in which union leadership, the bargaining relationship, and hence the 'drama of negotiation' could be dramatically affected by significant change within the managerial structures, priorities and strategies of an organisation. We also look at how the maintenance and mobilisation of collective support reflects these changes and the expectations and experiences of the workforce. We contend that overall, successful mobilisation of collective support requires the industrial relations actors involved to 'play out' the appropriate drama. Such drama was clear within the union leaders' action at the lock companies, indeed, the convenor at LockCo referred specifically to such a view as seen in the quote above. However such dramas are not explored within the formal or conventional accounts of collective action.

Collective Action: a Conventional Account

The Wider Context

The time span of the lock research from the early 1980s to the late 1990s makes it particularly exciting and challenging because this period has also been one of significant change in the wider economic, political, legislative and ideological environment in Britain. Reflecting this, there is a large body of literature offering varying perspectives on the extent of change (Marsh, 1992; Millward et al., 1992; McIlroy, 1995; McInnes, 1987; Blyton and Turnbull, 1998; Hartley, 1992). Overall, perhaps the greatest changes have been anticipated to have occurred in the arena of collective action, and in particular, trade union collective action.

Dramatic change in collective workplace relations might be anticipated, with regard to trade unions, bearing in mind the weight of negative factors that the British trade union movement has faced since 1979. In Britain, this concerns the continuing legacy of the Conservative government's (under Margaret Thatcher) project aiming to shift the balance of forces in society radically and permanently in favour of capital in the economy and the Right in politics. Trade union power was undermined by a legislative offensive, a variety of economic and structural changes leading to a decline in traditionally unionised sectors of the economy, public encouragement of employers to abandon collective bargaining, and the rise of 'new' popular management concepts such as Human Resource Management, Total Quality Management and Employee Involvement (Greene, 1999).

The expectation might be that the general salience of trade unions for workers has declined as unions have become less powerful and less demonstrably effective both in the workplace and at national level. Another change that has been suggested is that the permeation of individualistic ideals into the culture of the British workforce has led to an erosion of collectivism and a move to more individualistic expectations: that British workplace collectivism is dead. Finally, as organisations have taken on more cooperative, unitary ideologies, workers have come to feel more attachment to and shared identity as the company rather than to sectional groups, leading to a decline in feelings of 'them and us'; workers against management. Thus there are threats of 'new individualism' and 'new collectivism' facing unions (Bacon and Story, 1996).

The Impact of the Wider Context

Looking at what has happened over the period, in order to compare this with rhetoric; there has been an undeniable decline in union membership since and large-scale survey evidence (Cully et al., 1999; Millward et al., 1992) charts a significant trend towards union derecognition. In addition, the scope of collective bargaining has narrowed and on a number of workplace issues, union representatives felt that they were given no information, let alone consulted, about events (Cully et al., 1999). There has also been a dramatic decline in the incidence of strikes (traditionally seen as an indicator of union power: Terry, 1986). Marsh (1992) sees shop stewards as taking a more defensive and cooperative attitude towards management in the face of an increasing threat of job losses and diminished union power. Several authors (Terry, 1989; Marchington and Parker, 1990) refer to the 'marginalisation' of shop stewards as a characteristic of the 1980s. A review of existing case study evidence (Terry, 1995, pp. 215–17) tends to support the analysis that shop stewards and their organisations have been weakened and marginalised and that stewards themselves are more vulnerable than they were in earlier periods.

However, overall, there is a lack of consensus in the literature as to the extent and nature of changes in British industrial relations. Many writers have pointed to the gap between the expectations generated by popular management concepts and union initiatives, and the practice of industrial relations (Legge, 1989). The gap is most significant in moving from the macro to the micro analysis. The precise form of any kind of 'new workplace' or new employment relations has been difficult to identify and has perhaps been most obscure in relation to local workplace settings (Ackers et al., 1996). Some writers have seen trade union organisation, where it continues to exist, as remaining resilient (McIlroy, 1998), while the 'onslaught of individualism' seems challenged by incidences of industrial action in both the public and private sector throughout the 1990s. In addition, survey evidence indicates that people are continuing to join trade unions for very traditional reasons (Waddington and Whitson, 1992).

There is also a lack of consensus about what trade unions should do in response to the challenges faced and what their role is in the new millennium, at least in Britain. Strategies have varied from making trade unions more attractive to individual members with initiatives that seem to encourage a more individualistic form of trade union membership, through to increasing strength by union merger (see Ackers et al., 1996 for a summary). Debate has thus focused around whether these kind of individual benefits have become more important to union members leading to a more individualistic commitment to trade unions (Kelly and Heery, 1994).

Apart from national initiatives, there has also been debate about how to reinvigorate collective action at workplace level (Fairbrother, 1989). Much of this debate has focused around the action of prominent union activists in the workplace (what may be called union leaders) (Kelly, 1998). The style and character of leadership can be seen to exert a critical influence on the way in which the union organisation is responsive to general membership aspirations and the way in which collective awareness and activism of the mass of workers is stimulated (Hyman, 1979; Barling et al., 1992) and surges and troughs in membership participation mobilised upon (Fosh, 1993). As Fosh argues:

> The careful choice of local leadership style can yield results even when members' expectations and situations are not the most favourable for the development of unionism (1993, p. 589).

In other words, the leadership style can mediate the negative effects of external factors that appear to undermine the position of trade unions.

Connected to such debates, the most recent strategies for renewal in Britain have focused around the need to develop an 'organising' culture within the trade union movement, drawing on similar trends within the trade union movements in the USA and Australia. Such a strategy has been actively promoted by the TUC with its Organising Academy, opened in 1998, which was established to produce a cadre of 'lead organisers' who can plan and manage organising campaigns and promote the cause of organising across the British trade union movement (Heery et al., 2000).

But many questions are left unresolved, most significantly, in what direction should trade union leaders be moving and organising their members? The debate seems to be polarised around whether or not unions should be aiming to highlight the shared interests that exist between management and union rather than basing relations on adversarialism (Darlington, 1994; Kelly, 1996). Should union leaders be aiming for Social Partnership (Ackers and Payne, 1998) or remaining militant (Kelly, 1996)? There is a significant lack of studies which attempt to draw out answers to these questions with in-depth analysis at the workplace level, with notable exceptions (Greene et al., 2000). John Kelly (1998; 1996) provides some generalised theorising, drawing upon Mobilisation Theory (Tilly, 1978) and finds union leadership to be critical in how and why union members are mobilised into taking collective action.

However there are still significant gaps in our knowledge, especially regarding the type of detailed analysis that ethnography helps provide. As John Kelly states: 'we know a great deal about the structure and scope of bargaining … by contrast, our knowledge of the bargaining *process* is astonishingly slight' (1998, p. 17). We still have little understanding about why and how individual union leaders decide upon particular strategies and what the impacts are of such strategies upon membership activism and willingness to act collectively.

Possible Ways Forward

The impact of the wider industrial relations influences and possible ways forward and areas of renewal for trade unions, must therefore be set within the context of the work place, where influences may be mediated at the institutional level, by the specific unions, managers, workers and the companies with whom they deal. The foregoing discussion is relevant to a view of the need for in-depth accounts such as the lock ethnographies. Firstly, the longitudinal comparison at LockCo provided an opportunity to assess the resilience of a workplace union organisation in face of the external threats and challenges presented. Secondly, the comparison between LockCo and KeyCo provided an opportunity to explore the way that differences can be explained by specific variation in managerial and union strategies at the two companies. Thus there are possible contingent or influencing factors in an analysis and explanation of employee perceptions of the employment relationship, which shed further light on the extent of change in the arena of collective action. What we aim to achieve in the next section is firstly, to establish the attachment that the lock workers feel and felt to their workplace union: did we for example see evidence of a decline of collective spirit or solidarity across the period? Secondly, given the nature of collective attachment, how did the union leaders in both LockCo and KeyCo choose certain strategies and what was their impact on mobilising collective action?

Collective Action: an Ethnographic Account

Trade union membership, and willingness to take industrial relations became an interesting defining feature of the two lock companies. Notably, as compared to views concerning other issues (such as towards the company, work, management), where the views of the lock workers at the two firms was generally quite similar, the divergence in attitudes with regard to the union was striking. The union was viewed consistently more unfavourably at KeyCo than at LockCo over a variety of issues, which challenges the generalised conclusions of conventional accounts by exploring how differences within ostensibly similar contexts can have significant effects on collectivist attitudes.

The Salience of Trade Unionism at the Lock Companies

The most striking difference, was the degree of negativity towards the union at KeyCo. Most KeyCo workers spoke negatively about their own union and unions in general. Many said that they did not know why they bothered continuing to be members. As one worker commented, 'I sometimes wonder why myself. I don't think I do derive any benefit from it to tell you the truth', while another added, 'Well I don't know why anyone bothers, they've never done anything for we.' This was in stark contrast to LockCo, where most saw their union as relevant and necessary, as one assembler remarked, 'I think it's the only thing the working class people have got. I think it's a very good thing. You can't really be without one.' In fact, looking at the longitudinal views across the period from the early 1980s at LockCo, the salience of the union to LockCo workers appeared to have increased, notably because the wider context had become much more unfavourable towards employees. In an increasingly unfavourable economic context, the union was seen as more relevant and necessary to ordinary members. Workers mentioned the unfavourable employment context more frequently in the late 1990s than in the early 1980s. Characteristics of this unfavourable context included: deteriorating employment rights vis-à-vis a stronger and less sympathetic management, a worsening wage situation; and declining job security within the wider context of high unemployment and wider market difficulties, including the threat to the industry of foreign imports. Overall, the most frequently mentioned reason for union membership was in order to balance the power of management. There was a clear impression that employees felt they had lost power in their relationship with management in a climate where their position was increasingly vulnerable. Thus one shopfloor worker commented: 'That's the only form of protection you've got against any management today', while another employee added: '... with the legislation that's recently been brought in, you do need a union to look after your interests, if you didn't they'd [management] just run over you.'

The importance of the union had thus become more apparent in the context of the characteristics of an unfavourable employment situation. Indeed, we were able to further confirm the ostensible support for trade union membership by comparing views at LockCo in the 1990s with those in the early 1980s. The pessimism of some of the workers themselves in 1983 as to the salience of the union was not carried over. In 1983, an industry closed shop[2] existed at LockCo, and there was a lot of opposition to this lack of choice, indeed, many lock workers stated that they would not have joined voluntarily and thought that a lot of people would drop out of the union if the closed shop ended. In addition, a substantial group in 1983 took the view that the union was, 'necessary rather than liked'. However this latent dissatisfaction did not seem to have materialised in the 1990s, where there was almost unanimous support for voluntary membership of the union. Indeed the law now requires that ballots for the use of check off are held (where membership subscriptions are paid through deductions from pay packets). The process for renewing check off at LockCo was held in January 1997 and was overwhelmingly successful with the loss of only one member and the gaining of 25 new members.[3] This again relates to overall continuity in attitude across the period, with gradual trends towards the union being seen as more salient in the changed context.

In comparison, at KeyCo, the experience of employees was of dissatisfaction with their union. Overall, this dissatisfaction appeared to centre on views that the union was powerless to help them, with people commenting that they felt that the union had lost power over the period from the early 1980s. Issues mentioned by KeyCo workers as demonstrating the lack of power included the inadequacy of union influence over the recent pay settlement (where a new bonus scheme was introduced which significantly reduced many employees' wages), and over job protection.

With regard to pay for example, at KeyCo, we gained the general feeling from workers that the union was not effective in increasing their pay. They were very dissatisfied with their pay, an issue discussed in Chapter Two, outlining the failure of the new bonus scheme, which had triggered a bonus at the lowest level only six times in the 20 months it had been in place. Workers at LockCo were as dissatisfied with their pay as those at LockCo, indeed looking across the period since 1983, there had been growing dissatisfaction (Greene, 1999). Wage structures within the company were seen to have generally become increasingly unfair: 'they're are asking people now to do things they've never done before and they're not being rewarded for the effort.' Where the grading structure was teamed with a merit system, this was seen as further evidence of management arbitrariness, and of a situation where favouritism and victimisation were endemic, as a group of men affected by the merit system commented: 'if your face fits, you're all right'; 'at times, its the colour of your eyes', or another: 'its a bit cap in hand, sort of ... you've got to beg for the rise.' However, at LockCo, dissatisfaction with pay and wider economic stability appeared to have led to pay remaining a prime reason for union membership. There had been a significant rise in the number of people mentioning pay as a reason for union membership, and people spoke to us of the importance of pay: '75 per cent of them [the union] being here, is to try and negotiate a decent standard of living for members', and 'I think for most people, that's the main criteria on which they judge the union.' LockCo employees in the 1990s had a clear understanding of the restrictions placed upon unions and the difficulties that officials and representatives face in negotiating wages and jobs in a difficult climate. They did not blame the union for the lack of success in pay settlements, but the structure of negotiations within the management/union Joint Industrial Council (JIC). As employees explained:

> ... we always seem to come out a lot worse than we expect ... I think it's not so much the union, I think their hands are tied because it's all to do with the JIC ... the smaller companies dictate what the likes of this company can get.

Employees pointed to the difficulties that the union faced in negotiating with an unsympathetic and harsh management. One compared the present situation to that under past management (reflecting the discussion in Chapter Two):

> In the past you could negotiate with the company ... now they argue and question the wording of agreements and they seem less honourable people to what they seemed years ago ... we've lost any initiative we had ... you're on the defensive all the while.

With regard to job protection, similar contrasts between views of effectiveness of the union were found. Indeed, one KeyCo worker had not joined the union specifically because the union could not protect jobs, 'I think it's a waste of time ... I mean what can they do? If they sack me tomorrow, they'll not get me my job back.' Most workers at LockCo were as pessimistic about the ability of the union to protect their jobs as they were at KeyCo, but most recognised the difficulty the union faced, believing that the union did what it could to protect jobs in the circumstances. In the early 1980s, a majority of the workers were confident in the union's ability to protect their jobs, with people commenting on how the union had fought to keep the apprentices' jobs and had moved people around, rather than see them be made redundant. As one shop steward commented then: 'We have done it in the last two or three years ... all our negotiations have been with that ... main consideration in everything that is done.' In contrast, a general view in the late 1990s was that while the union did not have particular success in protecting jobs and preventing redundancies, it did a good job in the circumstances. One worker commented:

> they always seem to make that their main argument in any case, whether it be wages, or general redundancies, when they have come about in the past, they seem to be very effective at protecting jobs as far as they can possibly go.

At LockCo in the late 1990s, most people believed that the union was not effective over job protection, but did not blame the union, instead seeing the situation as arising due to the dominance of management in the employment relationship: 'Not effective I'm afraid ... nothing's secure today, you know it's, I mean they try, but at the end of the day, he that pays the piper calls the tune.' In contrast, employees at KeyCo laid blame squarely at the feet of the union, commenting that the union had 'let them down'. An example of the common viewpoint was:

> At one time, the union used to fight for redundancies, now the company says 'Ten people are being made redundant' and the next week they're out the door, never see the union step in now.

Collective Action at the Lock Companies

On the theme of industrial action, divergence between the two companies was equally clear. At LockCo, everyone we spoke to supported the principle of a right to strike. In comparison, at KeyCo, employees were divided and a substantial minority did not support the right to strike. Opposition to industrial action stemmed primarily from feelings that striking did not accomplish anything for the workers; indeed many gave examples of the way in which the strike in 1990 had not led to an improved pay deal, but had only meant lost pay for those days they were on strike: 'Striking, I don't think it accomplishes anything ... in the end, it's the workers who suffer' and 'It's no good striking these days, everybody is in the same boat and the strike will not do anyone any good.' In addition, many at KeyCo thought that people would not show support for industrial action compared to only one person at LockCo (albeit as a last resort). The reasons offered for this lack of support included the barriers of legislation, the predominantly female workforce (who were seen as less militant), fear of losing jobs and lack of collective feeling. Two

KeyCo workers related a recent demonstration of the lack of support for the union, when industrial action was proposed over the pay settlement:

> The union man, he got everyone together and he says 'Right, before I can do anything at all, what I want is a show of hands to see who would be willing to take industrial action' ... I reckon a quarter of hands went up ... I'm afraid the old people power for the union wasn't there.

This story was reiterated by another KeyCo worker:

> We had a meeting about them taking the money off these people and the union came down, they had us all outside to talk about it, but they hadn't got 100 per cent backing so of course they couldn't do anything about it. A union is only as good as its members.

There was a completely contrasting view at LockCo where there was unanimous support for the right to strike in the 1990s, an increase in feeling since 1983, when a small minority had not supported the right. However, it should be noted that employees then and now, were very concerned that strikes should be used 'sparingly and moderately' and would only be deemed necessary as a last resort, over 'important issues'. Typical comments in the 1980s were: 'The ultimate weapon, the H bomb sort of thing', and 'I can't see much point in striking unless it's something that's really serious.' These were echoed by comments in the 1990s: 'not to strike over every thing that comes up but I think if an issue is strong enough', and, 'strike action should always be used as a last resort'. The concerns of the shopfloor were obvious, indeed at a shopfloor meeting that we attended,[4] support for the union in the pay negotiations was given but some people were concerned to point out that an offer of their support did not equate with support form a strike. The convenor then had to outline various aspects of collective support that could be given short of striking (such as overtime bans, short term stoppages) in order to reassure them.

However, whilst workers only wanted to utilise industrial action as a last resort, there were a number of occasions in the 1990s when groups of LockCo workers felt that the last resort measure was necessary, compared to the lack of success that the union leaders had in generating support for collective action at KeyCo. One example included a one-hour stoppage of work by all employees in protest at changes to sick pay arrangements in 1997. Another involved a situation where management had unilaterally changed the piecework values on an assembly line in 1998 without first consulting the union, and the employees in that area refused to work to the new values, suffering a drop in earnings by reverting to unmeasured pay. The success of this united action was demonstrated when the company completely reversed their policy and reinstated the old values. Such an example also challenges the explanations at KeyCo for lack of support for industrial action because of the female workforce, given that the assembly line that took this industrial action at LockCo was all women.

Workplace Union Democracy: Communication, Accountability and Representativeness

Once again, there was significant divergence in attitudes between the companies. In general, members at KeyCo were not satisfied with the level of communication that they had with their union representatives and officials and the amount of information they received about union business. Many people commented on how they feel that shop stewards 'fobbed them off', alluding to a feeling that union business was kept secret from members: 'They have their monthly meetings, but nine times out of 10, you hear things through hearsay … you go and ask the union and they say "Oh we don't know".' Another KeyCo worker related her frustration at the lack of communication between the union representatives and the ordinary members: 'If I didn't go out of my way to ask, I'd never know … I'd say "Well tell me all about it", "Er can't. It's still secret".'

In comparison, a large majority of workers at LockCo had positive views of the communication process within the lock union. Looking more closely at the discourse, complaints from the two companies focus around different issues. At LockCo, those few who were not satisfied, complained that individual stewards did not tell them things as part of usual practice. At KeyCo, members complained that even if they went to their stewards themselves and asked specifically for information, they did not receive it and that they felt shut out from the process.

A similar situation existed with regard to the issue of how accountable the union was to members. Again, the balance of opinion was much more negative at KeyCo than at LockCo. Most at KeyCo did not feel that their views were reflected in union action, compared to only one person we spoke to at LockCo. Many at KeyCo felt that union representatives and officials had their own opinions and made decisions without regard to members' views. As one person commented:

> In times gone past ... the union used to come back and say to the shopfloor, 'We've received a proposal from the management and we put it to you on the shopfloor', it was up to the shopfloor to accept that or reject it. But they seem to forget that now, it's already decided.

Another added:

> I don't know where they get their ideas from ... it was something they'd thought off the top of their heads, they want it, asked for it, and got it, but nobody's asked for it. I think that's a lack of coordination between the union and the workforce.

This was in stark contrast to LockCo, where most workers we spoke to felt that the union did represent their interests well and that union action did reflect their opinions, channelled through the shop stewards. An emphasis on the need for the union to remain accountable was apparent in the recognition by the convenor, after discussion with his shop stewards, that he had made a mistake when he had neglected to offer a ballot on the pay settlement to a company site in Birmingham.[5] While there were only 50 people at the site so their ballot would not have made impact on the result of the wider poll, he realised that it had been a mistake not to offer them a ballot on principle and went to the site to make a formal apology and listen to the complaints made by members.

Union-Management Relationship

Perhaps the most damning views of the union at KeyCo were those which saw the union as supporting management rather than the workers; something which was not present in the LockCo workers' discourse. Indeed, a large minority at KeyCo felt the union was on 'management's side'. Common views included statements such as:

> Before the union was behind the workers but now the union seems to be something more management ...

> The union, especially here, is being run by the company ... the union bend the rules to suit the company, not the workers.

> I mean they're in their pockets.

One member at KeyCo even thought that the union had been bribed by management with shop stewards having been given higher paying jobs:

> most of the shop stewards here, for some reason, they all got put on a grade two, to keep them quiet, so they can say 'Your pay's higher than everyone else's.' Well they've got them over a barrel.

Employees at KeyCo clearly thought that their union leaders and representatives were incorporated into the management world view, agreeing to policies that they saw as undermining their interests (Rollinson, 1991; Black and McCabe, 1998).

Overall, the workplace union organisation at KeyCo was viewed consistently more unfavourably than at LockCo. Similar views at both companies might have been anticipated, bearing in mind the community-based nature of the national union, and the historical and sociological similarities between the firms. We tried to explain the divergence by exploring two propositions. Firstly, that we needed to look more closely at the individual company contexts: that the divergence in views was due to the particular local and historical traditions of union organisation at each firm. Secondly, that while in-plant structures of the union organisation are similar at each firm, the nature of union leadership (the drama played out by union leaders in their interactions with managers and employees) has an impact upon the terms of engagement between the union and management, and the way in which these terms are viewed by members.

The Local and Historical Traditions of Union Organisation

Commitment and attitudes towards the union will ultimately be influenced by members' experience of the union structure and processes (Fosh, 1993). Here we draw on the longitudinal evidence at LockCo. Longitudinal exploration was not available for KeyCo, but we were able to speak to the previous incumbent of the union convenorship, full time officials of the union who had held their positions for over 10 years, and could draw on the memories of long service employees. The ex-convenor commented on the strength of the union at KeyCo, with a full time convenor's position, shop stewards for each department, weekly shop stewards' meetings, and departmental works council arrangements where employee representatives would meet with management. The ex-convenor also indicated his successful personal working relationship with the Personnel Director leading to advances such as the introduction of a new piecework system, the introduction of a system to reduce the amount of redundancies and the introduction of a company wide wage negotiation to replace the existing departmental wage negotiations. This matched the historical background at LockCo, which saw the evolution of the full time convenor's role in the 1970s and a similarly strong shop steward network. The union occupied a central position in both companies, recognised by management for traditional collective bargaining of wages and terms and conditions. Both workplace organisations rested on highly informal relations with management. Other than wage bargaining and a 'bare bones' four stage agreement for disciplinary procedures, little was committed to paper and most negotiations were conducted through informal chats and rested on a high trust, personal relationship between the convenor and Personnel Managers.

The personal nature of union leadership resources may also be relevant to understanding the process and outcomes of negotiations, in other words, incumbents to positions of influence can gain advantages and disadvantages from traditions built up by their predecessors (Batstone et al., 1977). At KeyCo the convenor was female, and one might anticipate problems in a union organisation traditionally dominated by men. However, while she perceived some opposition as a female convenor, especially from the tool room (the founding area of the union and that seen historically to be the most militant), her position had never been openly challenged and she was elected unopposed. She also related how she had threatened to resign soon after she was elected in 1990 and was persuaded to stay on by a show of support through a shopfloor petition. Women have also played a major role in the national union organisation since the early 1970s, with a female President elected in 1974. The workforce in the industry has also come to include far more women over the period since the 1970s. Overall the union organisation at KeyCo was no weaker historically than at LockCo.

As discussed in Chapter Two, the working relationship between convenor and Personnel Director at KeyCo had become more formalised since the corporate take-over in 1988, and no longer had the personal characteristics it had done in the past. This was seen by the KeyCo convenor as a symptom of a deterioration in the relationship. Moreover, the position of the convenor ceased to be full time in 1998. By contrast, the convenor continued to hold a full time position at LockCo. While both companies had maintained their steward/member ratios from the 1980s, LockCo continued to have the better ratio. In some respects, the union at KeyCo had thus come to occupy a less central and weakened institutional position in recent years. However, while members' views and opinions of the union were probably influenced by the weakness of the union's current situation, this was a relatively recent development and does not provide a persuasive explanation for the divergence in attitudes of members. Other possible explanations must therefore be explored which look at the particular recent circumstances, in the light of embedded experiences and the leadership styles of the convenors.

The Nature of Union Leadership

Referring back to the quote which opens this chapter, the trade union convenor at LockCo noted that, 'a lot of my role and interaction is theatre', suggesting how the terms of engagement between management and union can be seen as a drama. In relevance to the discussion in this chapter, the view is that if the union can persuade the membership that it has done all it can to protect the interests of employees, and has made some demonstrable advances, the members will stay supportive of the union even if the company still faces sweeping work reorganisation and 'unavoidable' redundancies. In other words, the union representatives needed to 'play their appropriate parts'.

LockCo had begun to face similar restructuring to that which had been experienced at KeyCo, however the shop stewards and members did not feel as did those at KeyCo, that the union was on 'management's side'. A different situation was found at KeyCo where people felt that the union had 'sold us down the river' and this was reflected in their opinions of the union as being 'on management's side'. This related to the feelings voiced by members that the union was powerless to help them and has had little demonstrable effect in the workplace.

At KeyCo the emphasis was on a different type of 'performance', a very public cooperation with management, with the convenor sharing the view of managers that the work organisation changes will be good for the workforce. The terms of engagement between the union and management have therefore been managed differently at KeyCo. The proposition here, is that the divergence in attitudes towards the workplace union can be explained in part, by variations in the social and relational processes of union organisation (within the context of changing managerial strategies and structures); most notably communication within the union, involvement and participation of members in union business, and the degree of separation between union leaders and rank and file. This in turn influences the way in which the union meets (or engages) with management and how this engagement is viewed by members.

Attitude Towards Restructuring

The gap between the views of the convenor and those of the rank and file at KeyCo was evident. For instance, with regard to the restructuring programme introduced by the new owner, the convenor supported restructuring, feeling that it would yield significant gains for employees. As she commented:

> I want to change, I like the changes and I think we're changing for the right. Whereas the shopfloor want stopping with the piece work and are quite happy how we used to be. I think they see me in management's purse at the minute … because I'm convinced we're going the right way … I'll stick it out and prove it to them that I'm right.

Moreover, the convenor was frustrated with the rank and file's opposition to the restructuring:

> all they'm interested in is gloom and doom. I lose patience with them, they talk so much rot most of the time. It's not that they've got a genuine reason for not wanting the move, it's just 'cos they want to do their job. There's no pleasing them to be honest.

The convenor was similarly critical of her shop stewards and did not feel confident in delegating duties to them, relating past experiences where they were unable to carry out fairly simple duties. The convenor at LockCo also noted this lack of delegation by his counterpart, commenting that full time officer's reports indicated that a lot of their time was taken up by dealing with domestic issues at KeyCo which he would have passed onto shop stewards to deal with. Furthermore, the convenor at KeyCo appeared unwilling to use her shop stewards for the purposes of information dissemination, as she stated: 'We do Photostat the minutes but any major issues I prefer to announce them myself because I just can't trust them to get the message across in the right way.' In comparison, the LockCo convenor was not convinced that the restructuring would yield benefits for members and in this, he demonstrated a different view to that of the convenor at KeyCo. While she was convinced that the changes are for the good of members, the LockCo convenor did not feel positively about the proposals. As a diary entry of 10 October 1997 revealed:

> When attending a meeting such as today's, one is left with feelings of no pride. Where is the Department of Trade and Industry now these job losses are

> announced. Should they not be saying to [the multinational], 'you assured us that your purchase of LockCo would be good for the industry'. The acquisition may be good for the shareholders ... but for the people of LockTown, it is another hammer blow to an already beleaguered industry.

At LockCo, there appeared to be significant mutual support between the convenor, the stewards and the members, reflected in the expressions of trust which members voiced and the support and cheery optimism demonstrated at shop steward's committee meetings. Despite the changes proposed by the management at LockCo (particularly bearing in mind the scale of restructuring that had already occurred at KeyCo), the general atmosphere at the shop stewards' committee meeting immediately following the announcement of restructuring in October 1997 was cheery and optimistic. This was not because people were any happier about the proposals at LockCo than they were at KeyCo. Indeed, stewards were very concerned about the scale of redundancies proposed and the impact of the abolition of piecework on earnings. Rather, it was because there was confidence that the union (particularly in the form of the convenor) would fight for the best interests of the workers. As one female shop steward remarked: 'So the situation is, we're not going to let [the multinational] come into LockCo like they did at KeyCo, we're not going to let them roll over the union.' In return, the support that he received from the membership gave him the confidence to stand up to management. He was thus confident that the union could resist any equalisation of terms and conditions across the two firms, which would negatively affect his members at LockCo.

Leadership Style

Overall, the convenor at LockCo demonstrated a far more participatory and collectivist style than the KeyCo convenor. At LockCo, there appeared to be more consistency in terms of interpretation of this 'script' and willingness to act collectively as a result, than at KeyCo. The LockCo convenor deliberately aimed to increase the flow of information to members. One of the senior shop stewards produced what came to be known as 'John's unofficial minutes' of the shop stewards' committee meeting, which were pinned up on the company notice board as soon as the meeting ended, preceding distribution of the official minutes later in the week. The convenor was also concerned that union representatives were seen as accountable to the membership and not hiding information. The convenor briefed the shop stewards that they should never act secretively:

> We are not a secret society, we will not say 'No comment', but whenever we can, we will give as much information as we are able to and if any members have any queries beyond that, they should come and speak to me.

He recognised that members were likely to be anxious about the proposed changes, and worried for their jobs. The message for stewards was to retain a united front, and to instil confidence in the members, 'We must remain upbeat and optimistic about things, if you all have a depressed attitude, it will not achieve anything for the members.' Such an attitude was reinforced by the convenor's diary entries such as this one of 14 October 1997:

> Once again the morale at this factory is very low. Both the workers and the managers felt concerned with regard to their future and once again it was up to us to be positive. Being positive in this context is all about being clear, members want answers and we should be able to provide that service.

The confidence and optimism appeared quite infectious at the meetings and lead to a rallying round of support behind the union. When discussing the tactics for opposing a new redundancy scheme, the shop stewards engaged in some morale boosting, with one shop steward proclaiming his support for the convenor shouting, 'We'll follow you to the end of the road', which was followed by clapping and cheering across the room. The LockCo union also attempted to be representative of members' views. The proceedings of committee meetings were full of comments, inquiries and questions from the rank and file membership, indicating how the opinions of ordinary members were filtered through to the representative bodies (Cohen and Fosh, 1988).

The LockCo convenor also made a point of delegating important issues. One example was the formation of a subcommittee to negotiate new holiday arrangements. Moreover, the shop stewards were a check on the convenor taking on too much. At one committee meeting, a shop steward commented that he thought the convenor was overworked and should set up a subcommittee to deal with the redundancy negotiations; which was agreed to. The lay membership and shop stewards thus had some defining role on policy and placed some limitations on the autonomy of the convenor, indicating that more of a 'two-way' relationship existed, as compared with KeyCo. Members were willing to rally around in support of the union, demonstrated in the overwhelming acceptance by the workforce of the proposal for work organisation changes at a mass meeting. Members also seemed willing to make a stand against management, in actually taking industrial action when necessary.

In Chapter Two we discussed the disappointment which workers felt about the deterioration in the labour/management relationship. Overall, workers wanted to have more say and involvement in the decisions made about their working lives. Personal contact, the human element of paternalism, was an important part of the embedded expectations of the employment relationship at the lock companies. Similarly, the personal contact of the union at LockCo was praised. The majority of people in 1996 had a positive view of communication channels within the union. People mentioned the accessibility of the union and how the local site of the union made communication easier than in larger unions:

> 'I think it's the geography of the place that helps more than anything. It is easier, a lot more easier to contact Bellamy House which is situated in Willenhall than it would the AEU' and, 'It's a good little union ... as regards it's a localised place, and with locks, it's a localised thing, so I think you can get things across more easily without having to battle ... say with the giants, which seem so remote'.

Many spoke positively about the accessibility of the union, commenting on the ease of communication with officials and the ability for quick action:

> It is a union that's in the dead centre of town and 95 per cent of its members revolve around that centre ... it can be called on at any time, it's within easy reach.

With regard to community involvement, there was a generally positive opinion of the involvement of the union outside of the workplace at LockCo, which can be compared with the generally negative views of the role of the company and management (see Chapter Two). Activities that were mentioned included, Family Fun Days, union dances, sports sponsorship, charity sponsorship, the lock museum, celebrations for the union's fiftieth anniversary, company perks such as sick leave and a political role with local MPs. Many commented that such union events were popular; indeed tickets for the Valentine's Dance in 1996 sold out and there was a waiting list. The LockCo convenor was also keen to take on some of the community responsibilities which the company had relinquished. A prime example was the union taking over the running of the Locks Welfare Society when the company withdrew support. It had thus become the union's role to take on the mantle of campaigning for the maintenance of facilities that hark back to the era of family paternalism such as the Social Club and the company canteen. In comparison, we can look back to Chapter Two at the views of workers towards management, and their disappointment in the lack of recognition of the importance of such traditions of paternalistic community involvement. In terms of the dramaturgical metaphor, there is evidence here of the different ways in which the social situation at the firm was 'framed' so as to 'shape the general perspective upon which information is presented and interpreted' (Gardner and Avolio, 1998, p. 41) and 'scripted', so as to define the scene and provide 'emergent guides for collective consciousness' (ibid.).

Union/Management Relations

At neither firm did an official apparatus exist for shop stewards and management to meet and, as discussed earlier, much of the negotiation rested on the informal personal relationship between the convenor and the personnel manager. There was thus an increased danger at both firms of this relationship being viewed by members as incorporated.

The convenor at KeyCo, commented on the close and cooperative relationship that she had with managers:

> I'm more involved than any other convenor has been, it's taken me a few years to get where I am with management, but we do avoid a lot of situations because they do sit down and talk to me now.

Further, she hinted at the kind of informal negotiation that went on between her and the personnel manager before the official negotiations begin, 'We'll talk about it first and then we'll start the official negotiations.' The convenor at LockCo also shared this approach, for example meeting the personnel director outside of the workplace, to thrash out the terms of the agreement, whilst the official pay negotiations were continuing.

The point to be reiterated however is that the terms of this cooperation with management at workplace level need to be carefully formulated if the support of members is to be maintained. It is a public drama acted out in the workplace. The 'performance' needs to be carefully 'framed' and 'scripted' (Gardner and Avolio, 1998; Goffman, 1959). The convenor at LockCo was very aware that he had to retain the 'drama' of some opposition to management, and the relationship between the union and management appeared far from amiable. This was shown in the 'notice board wars' with letters posted publicly between the convenor and the personnel manager, sometimes involving quite personal attacks, and illustrating their inability to talk face-to-face. The convenor and stewards had a generally sceptical view of management integrity, illustrated in their demands that all agreements and proposals be formally written rather than being based on oral 'gentlemen's agreements', which would have been the traditional method. They also indicated the failure of any management communications that have involved company wide presentations of proposed changes. These were seen as occurring too late in the process of change to afford employees any opportunity to participate or make useful comments. For the stewards, these only increased the need for the union to act as the official channel of communication. Members regarded evidence of conflict between managers and the union as a positive aspect of the relationship, and the convenor related how a member had praised him for 'having a good old go' at the Operations Manager on the shopfloor. The convenor, reported that they were just having a heated discussion about an issue, but that this was typical of the membership views. In this, the union convenor at LockCo was seen to be 'playing the appropriate part' as opposed to the situation at KeyCo.

The dual strategy of agreeing to engage with management while reassuring workers that the union is still independent and 'on their side' appears to have had success so far at LockCo. The union had been kept informed by management at most stages along the change process and had been able to demand the addition of beneficial clauses within the work reorganisation proposals, such as inclusion of training programmes. The communication channel between key managers and the union had become so embedded that in many cases, the union heard about a proposal or initiative before middle managers. Sometimes, senior managers used the LockCo convenor as the sole communication channel to employees, completely bypassing management levels. While the convenor at LockCo had a very informal relationship with the management, this did not mean that managers had the power to dictate to him or the union. The convenor had been able to control the timing of meetings, demanding that representatives of the SSC are present, resisting unreasonable demands from management to meet them at inconvenient times and places or when notice had been too short. This led to managers agreeing to reorganise such meetings. One incident involved the rescheduling of an important meeting, called at very short notice, because the convenor had already planned to attend his daughter's 'parent-teacher' night at school. The union thus did not appear to engage with management in a way that suggested a one-sided relationship or where the union could be said to be incorporated. The nature of the engagement between the union and management thus has an impact on how effective the union is able to be in terms of negotiation. The terms of engagement had been controlled at LockCo, objectively by not becoming subservient to management's agenda, and subjectively, by a public demonstration of independence and principled opposition.

In contrast, the convenor at KeyCo lacked the same degree of influence in setting either the agenda or the pace of change. She commented that while they did communicate easily when they were in meetings and negotiations, it was very difficult for her to get hold of managers to talk to them. Often she felt that managers used her deliberately to undermine other managers, giving her key information before managers in order to embarrass them. It is interesting to see the difference in perceptions of the same situation by the two convenors. At LockCo, the convenor saw this as evidence of the strength of the union as a communication channel, while at KeyCo, the convenor felt that this undermined her position. The irony of the KeyCo case is worth noting, in that while the convenor is criticised by members for being a management stooge, she was also treated with a degree of contempt by KeyCo management; indeed the union had become increasingly enfeebled at KeyCo.

These comparisons between the two companies suggest that effective moderate trade union leadership needs a careful construction and public presentation of relations. It is this that is an influence on shaping the views of workers towards their union. The union representatives at LockCo, had more of an entrenched position institutionally with management than did the union organisation at KeyCo. At LockCo, the union was a party to management decision-making and consultation meetings and was seen as a vital communication channel. However, this had not led to a loss of member support because there was still evidence that the union representatives had not taken on the management world-view, in contrast to how the union was perceived at KeyCo.

Structure and Consciousness

In order to discuss possible alternative explanations for understanding the findings, it should be noted that coexisting alongside the changes in union leadership style, are obviously, managerial strategies and priorities. At KeyCo, management had restructured their work organisation far more profoundly than at LockCo. As discussed earlier, as part of this work restructuring, management had also (intentionally or otherwise), restructured the basis of their relationship with the union, effectively denying an independent role for unionism. We have thus drawn out the fact that the particular union leadership style is integral to the effectiveness of the union in negotiations and in maintaining membership support. However, at KeyCo, having faced dramatic change earlier, the ability of the convenor to present herself as performing a useful and independent job had been significantly reduced. Within a wider context of trade union weakness, perhaps the ability of a union leader to display their independence may relate more to management's preparedness to allow the union to do this.

However, this is not sufficient as an explanation. The issue here is that while the reorganisation had only just began at LockCo, the same radical change was inevitable and the new management team were now from the same owning corporation to that at KeyCo. Despite this, there were differences in the ways that each union leader approached the 'drama of negotiation'. While unions often are forced to operate on a terrain that is largely defined by managerial preference, unions can still choose to respond in different ways.

The ethnographic inquiry at the lock companies has highlighted the interplay between structure and consciousness where the person is both a creator and object of their situation. The evidence indicated how the personal leadership style of the convenor at LockCo encouraged the participation of stewards and members and succeeded in generating the active support of rank and file on a number of occasions. Conversely, the leadership style of the convenor at KeyCo had engendered the apathy of both her stewards and members as they became increasingly excluded from union processes. Perhaps more significantly, the convenor at KeyCo became detached from the views and concerns of her members, and increasingly came to see the terrain of issues bargained over by herself on behalf of her members as defined by the company. The point of interest here is that at KeyCo we find the convenor was creating and reinforcing a situation, which simultaneously, she felt a victim of. However, this should not be read as demonstrating the fact that the union leaders at the two workplaces were simply victims of circumstance. This is in line with the argument of Walton and McKersie (1965, p. 9), that people act purposefully within the context of labour negotiations. As part of interaction within the employment relationship, the purposeful action of the union leaders (what Walton and McKersie would call 'chief negotiators') is emphasised:

> a position which has influence and is instrumental in achieving results … moreover, even with respect to the potential influence he does possess, he must choose and time his tactics wisely (ibid., p. 282).

There is much to support the view that management at the two firms were similar in orientation and strategy, although the fieldwork was carried out when the firms were in different states of reorganisation. However, the evidence does point to the influence of the union leader at the two firms. Differences in managerial policy at LockCo (and their preparedness to allow the union to have an independent role), can be explained partly by the different way that the union leader engaged in the social situation of the employment relationship, which in turn affected members' attitudes, and so on.

Returning to the discussion of the specific way the two convenors played out their 'roles', Batstone et al. (1977) developed a typology of union representatives, of which the major distinction was between whether the union representative was considered to be a 'representative' or a 'delegate' leader. The 'delegate' has the mandate by members to do no more than carry out their wishes. The alternative view is that the union leader can be a 'representative', where a leadership role is adopted and policies are not only executed according to the wishes of membership, but initiatives are taken and policies autonomously. Both convenors at the lock companies could be seen as 'representative', rather than 'delegate' union leaders in that they both took initiatives and made policies autonomously. However, they were different kinds of representatives. At KeyCo, a situation had arisen where there was a 'vicious circle', where members had become apathetic about their union organisation and while complaining about the lack of accountability of their convenor, they did little to ensure there was more union democracy. In the end, they effectively allowed the convenor to act in the way that she did, largely through lack of action. In turn the convenor reinforced this situation, building on her experience of the apathy of the membership, which in turn legitimised her stance. At LockCo the convenor had in practice a similar level of autonomous control. However, there was more evidence perhaps of a 'virtuous circle', where the convenor effectively had the mandate of membership and where their experience led them to trust that he would act in their best interests. Thus we suggest, countering the alternative discussed above, that the union leader at KeyCo, while facing a context that was detrimental to independent unionism, can also be seen to have contributed to the lack of an independent role which the union held in the company. This also relates to an explanation of the continued resilience of the union organisation and maintenance of a view that the union was salient despite external negative factors in the wider context. As Ackers et al. (1996) emphasise, it is at the workplace level that the contours of British industrial relations are shaped. Here, union leadership styles and members' experiences of union action or inaction can mediate the impact of negative factors on the wider trade union movement.

Managing Social Partnership

In summary, in order for the union to maintain credibility with members, the truism that the way in which the union engages with management has to be carefully considered, is highlighted. These findings complement literature on this issue, emphasising that any practice of 'Social Partnership' cannot be only on management's terms (Kelly, 1996, 1998; Ackers and Payne, 1998). Management were adamant that the restructuring they proposed would take place at both companies, and trade unions find themselves with limited room for manoeuvre when the changes are seen as necessary for the survival of the company. However, 'necessity' can be seen as socially defined, where the world views of management and unions are developed in their interactions with each other. It is this that defines what is possible or desirable in which particular circumstances. Cooperation with management may be a prerequisite, for the trade union to have any influence on the way in which change is brought about. However, most lock workers still felt that there was a conflict of interests between workers and management, which the union must be seen to recognise, if they are not to be perceived as incorporated. Cooperation need not equate to 'incorporation', but cooperation without access to competing 'world views' and countervailing pressures, may lead to a view that the union is incorporated. Here, KeyCo workers' views of the union leaders as having taken on the 'world view' of management was an important factor in their negativity towards and lack of commitment to, the union. At a wider level, this viewpoint is clear in the TUC rhetoric of Social Partnership. The basis for partnership is on participation around common interests centred on corporate success and employment security, which remains firmly embedded in a pluralist and collectivist tradition, eschewing a simple identity of interest between employer and workforce (Ackers and Payne, 1998; Monks, 1996). The LockCo convenor also reflected this position when he stated:

> the traditional trade unionist cannot function in modern industrial situations. It's not about confrontation now, it's not adversarialism. We'll never be corporate partners, we'll always have conflict, but we need to be able to know how these companies operate, we need to be able to understand and talk in their language.

At LockCo, the unions' oppositional stance did not appear to have weakened their position but led to management being more careful about consulting and involving the union and appears to have led to significant bargaining gains for members. Certainly, at the time of research, it was early days in the negotiation process at LockCo, but so far the convenor appeared to have negotiated a relationship which while accepting cooperation, did not deny the existence of a basic conflict of interest.

The Relevance of Collective Action to Developing World Industrial Relations

There are a variety of reasons why the trade union movements and other collective solidarity organisations and groups in the developing world should be given a greater prominence in research on work. Firstly, the interest comes from the wider 'part' that the trade union movement has often played in many developing world contexts. Secondly, there are areas of shared concerns: we can highlight how the representation and protection roles of trade unions are key in maintaining and improving conditions for workers in the developing world, in exactly the same way as they are important in the developed.

Trade unions have tended to act as participants within wider social movements and have therefore played a prominent part in the development of many nations in the developing world. The context of Sub-Saharan Africa for example, sees many unions being part of wider movements for the installation of viable democratic governments. The Association of African Trade Unions had strong traditions of political action and was seen alongside various nationalist and pro-independence movements. Thus, in Africa, unionisation was often aided and promoted by the nationalist struggle for independence. Similarly, rights to free trade union membership are often part and parcel of the democratisation of the political process and become symbolic of a more liberal government. Recently, we have experienced the joint action of trade unions and employers in protest against political oppression in Zimbabwe (*Guardian*, 2 August 2000).

It is clear from only cursory viewing, that working conditions in many developing countries are particularly harsh and the individual has even less power and influence in the employment relationship. The South Korean example provides us with evidence of the mass exploitation of the working class as an aid to development (Bello and Rosenfeld, 1990; Wilkinson, 1994). Labour emerged as the key actor of production in the programme of export-oriented growth pushed by the Korean military-technocratic elite. Building competitive advantage was based on keeping labour cheap: from the 1960s until the Grand Labour Offensive in 1987, the wages of Korean workers were consistently lower than those of workers in Singapore, Taiwan and Hong Kong.

In 1987 the hourly pay of Korean manufacturing workers was 11 per cent of that in the USA and 14 per cent of that in Japan (Bello and Rosenfeld, 1990). The significance of such a comparison is that trade unions and collective action are seen as key to the possibility of improving conditions by forcing employers and government to change their strategies. One of the few recourses that workers in South Korea had was to take industrial action and there were a number of highly publicised industrial disputes at key workplaces from the mid-1970s. Textile industries had perhaps some of the worst conditions and the Chonggye Garment Workers Union became the symbolic centre of the nascent Korean labour movement, despite being an illegal organisation. Their actions were marked by a creative combination of self-sacrifice and confrontation, where representatives resorted to hunger strikes, sit-ins and even suicides to make their cause heard (ibid.). Ending the state repression of trade unions (under General Park from 1961–87) thus was a key part of the policies of the new regime in 1987 under Roh Tae Woo and his democratisation decree saw the number of trade unions double. It also opened the door to a flood of demands from the working class and industrial disputes in what became known as the Grand Labour offensive involving over seven thousand individual disputes. Immediate gains included minimum wage legislation and reduction in working hours.

Trade union membership (and independent trade union membership in particular) is similarly seen by Grace (1990) as a key force for improving standards for workers in Malaysia, with her case study focusing particularly on women electronics workers. Overall, trade unions are seen as one of the 'checks and balances against the arbitrary and capricious use of power by government' (Fosh, 1997). Trade unionism and collective action thus have remained a key feature of developing world industrial relations.

However, it should also be noted that decline in trade union membership is a world wide phenomenon, and that the fastest growing areas in many economies either have a limited trade union presence or are union free (for example in Asia: textiles, clothing and footwear) (Macdonald, 1997). One thus needs to consider whether industrial relations should embrace other collective movements and self-organising movements, some of which we discuss later.

In addition, trade unions still face opposition and repression in many developing world countries. For example, despite the utility of the trade union movement to the emergence of independent governments in many African countries, the post-Independence era has not necessarily seen the same level of interaction and rapport with many African governments. Various unions have suffered repeated repression from their governments who appeared to have perceived them as competitors and adversaries, in much the same way as they were perceived in 1980s Britain. In Nigeria unions were involved in the abortive democratisation process, which led to the dismissal of the pro-democracy union leaders by the military junta in 1994. While unions played a key role in the election of the Zambian President and a former trade union leader Frederick Chibula, when he became President, he quickly took measures against trade unions. Similar repression has been noted above in South Korea, and while gains were made during the Grand Labour Offensive from 1987–90, the business-backed government returned initially to repression, declaring the new militant Korean TUC illegal in 1990. Labour legislation has tended to uphold harsh conditions and increase employer power (Wilkinson, 1994) and there have also been continuing incidences of industrial action in South Korea throughout the 1990s. Grace (1990) reports on the restrictions placed on trade union membership in Malaysia, where electronics workers for example were only permitted to join trade unions (and then only company in-house unions) in 1988. Fosh (1997) offers examples of government restriction and opposition in Hong Kong. The interesting comparison here between many developing world countries and Britain, is that in contrast to the freedom enjoyed by many other European trade union movements, that in Britain is heavily regulated by the government. The political, economic, ideological and social climate of Britain from the 1970s has been one of adversity for trade unions as it has for movements in many developing world countries. Thus perhaps such trade union movements can learn from each other (ibid.).

In particular, it is interesting to point to reasons why trade unions have survived in the face of widespread adversity and why workers continue to campaign for their rights to join independent trade unions. While trade union membership may overall be declining, union density is obviously not the only indicator of trade union power and influence.

What is clear in this regard, is that we know even less about the process of gaining mobilisation and the actions of activists and members engaged in collective action in the developing world than we do in the developed. Voiced accounts about what union activists actually *do* and how they cope with the adversity facing them is scarce. In 1977, Ramaswamy stated 'there is not a single satisfactory account of how a union actually goes about its job' (1977, p. 7). Essentially, his frustration was that we know very little about unionism at grass roots level, or at the level of workplace analysis such as that which was afforded by the lock ethnographies. It is clear however that the frustration which he voiced in the late 1970s is still very potent today. The industrial relations field has moved forward in this direction only minimally in the developed world and even less so in the developing, where we have already established there is a dearth of voiced accounts. In the next section, we point to some rare examples of the type of voiced accounts around collective action and use them to suggest a way forward for industrial relations studies in this regard.

Moving the Debate Forward: Authentic Voices, Authentic Accounts (III)

The Need for Micro-level Studies

Our first suggestion for moving the debate about mobilisation and collective action forward in the industrial relations context, is that there is a need for micro-level studies which aim to present, with voiced accounts and ethnographic detail, the experience of those involved in mobilising and participating in collective action at work in a developing world context. Kapferer's (1972) study provides us with a rare example of a voiced account of the processes involved in negotiating and maintaining the employment relationship and mobilising collective action. He compares two periods within the study, the first when some militant activists failed to mobilise the workers for a walk out and the second, when other activists were successful in mobilising collective support. What Kapferer is really interested in is to look at the interactions and social transactions involved in generating these different situations in the two time periods. What is key to this analysis is a recognition of the importance of social relations to the mobilisation of collective action: 'individuals, in order to achieve the support of others must be able to manipulate and exert pressure through their sets of personal interactional relationships' (1972, p. 169).

Such assumptions can be related to our views of the existence of different dramas of the employment relationship. Kapferer's language of 'manipulation' resonates with a view of the need to deliberately 'frame' and 'script' social action so as to gain the desired effect through 'playing the appropriate part' which we draw out of the lock ethnographies. Within Kapferer's account, we begin to understand this role playing action through the characters and the voices of those individuals involved. For example, we follow the character of Lyashi, through his web of social interactions and begin to understand how important are these framed and scripted interactions to his rise to power, while that of the supervisors' declines. In a similar way, we traced the success of the

LockCo convenor in effectively framing his interactions, compared with those of the KeyCo convenor. What is clear, and which has been a continuous thread of argument within this volume, is that in order to maintain or generate support and commitment (whether we are concerned with workers, managers or trade union leaders) the appropriate 'part' in the appropriate drama must be played out. Within Kapferer's study, we gain a view of how various individuals presented themselves in relation to others in bids either to support their claims to authority or to impress others with their qualities: in essence, how they frame and script their interactions. Just as in the case of the LockCo convenor, we come to see how the successful mobilisation of collective action in the African textile factory needs the character of Lyashi to demonstrate effectiveness in gaining rewards for employees. What Chapters Two and Three have drawn out in particular, is that what is seen as appropriate is based on deeply embedded expectations. In the workplace of Kapferer's study, the sense of occupational community is clear as a determining feature of these expectations and which Lyashi has to recognise as important to the manipulation of social ties:

> the type of strategy pursued by employees in bargaining and negotiation with management was largely connected to the way they perceived various elements located in environment and organisation of these elements one to the other as these related to the worker situation (ibid., p. 333).

It is interesting then to look at Kapferer's account through the eyes of Buraways' (1974) critique, where he states that Kapferer places too much emphasis on the action of the activist leaders. Burawoy criticises the fact that the characters of Lyashi and Patel the supervisor are presented as free agents when in fact they face structural constraints. Indeed, it is obviously important that external contingencies are borne in mind: Ik Joo Hwang (1999) sees the lack of resistance from trade unions at the factories he studies in Korea as emerging from the threat of wider unemployment. However, reiterating our earlier assertions about necessity being socially constructed, ethnographic voiced inquiry allows us to move away from the bonds of structure to look more closely at processes. As in Kapferer's account, at the lock companies, the activist leader appears to take a very directing role in mobilising collective action. Social action is determined somewhat by the actions of management and wider external factors, but the lock ethnographies and Kapferer's account suggest that there are elements of 'choice' within these boundaries. What voiced accounts like these indicate are *why* and *how* certain choices are made.

We therefore tend to support Kapferer's assertions, but the fact that the lock study was conducted over a longer period of time allows us to take the analysis further than Kapferer's, being based around two close time periods. Walton and McKersie (1965) look specifically at the processes and interactions involved in labour negotiations between unions and management and they point to the difficulty that those individuals involved face in changing behavioural expectations of their wider organisational affiliations during labour negotiation situations. Their analysis pointed to procedures for 'tactical assignments' to lessen intraorganisational conflict as the negotiations took place (see ibid., pp. 312–40). However, our analysis in the lock companies extends upon this, pointing out that the employment relationship is in a constant process of negotiation, not just at particular moments of wage demands or grievance disputes for example (such as at Kapferer's textile factory). Thus, we saw the LockCo convenor taking action to 'frame', 'script' and 'perform' over a longer period of time, taking into consideration deeply embedded views, opinions and traditions of context. What is important is the everyday management of relations within their own organisations as well as when they specifically engage and interact with management.

If such a research agenda, which aims to put ethnographic detail at its heart, informed industrial relations studies more often, we would gain much more valuable accounts of how collective support is mobilised and maintained. For instance, Kramsjo and Wood's (1992) study of the activities of the self organised group Proshika in Bangladesh provides a useful chronicle of a variety of successful campaigns, where local campaigners have managed to mobilise groups of villagers to challenge the exploitation of local landowners and employers. The accounts provide information about *how* action is mobilised, through speaker meetings, collective legal claims, literacy training and the use of popular theatre. However, what is missing from these accounts is the *why* of the story: why campaigners chose the strategies they did and why villagers responded in a positive way to particular campaigns. For instance, themes emerging from the lock ethnographies and Kapferer's account might lead us to look for the 'fit' between the methods used by campaigners and local traditions and customs: in other words, finding appropriate parts in the appropriate dramas.

The Need for Studies of New Forms of Collective Action

Studies within developing world contexts involving collective support movements other than those that are directly work related, such as trade unions, are usually beyond the conventional arena of industrial relations, but offer valuable insights into the drama of collective activities.

For example, there are a number of accounts describing and analysing the activities of the Self Employed Women's Association (SEWA) based in India (see Rose, 1992; Kasturi et al., 1990), an action-oriented organisation designed to campaign to improve the conditions of the hundreds of thousands of self employed women. If we are looking for ways in which trade unions can renew and sustain themselves in the twenty-first century, after decades of derision and overt oppression, then perhaps movements such as SEWA present new models. As Rose (1992, p. 16) states:

> Under SEWA, women have forged a new model of what a trade union can be-a third world model, which defies conventional conception about who unions organise and what they do for their members.

Rose's account traces the history of SEWA, its emergence development and action programs, providing a view of an organisation which generates collective action across a very dispersed area and extends bargaining and campaigning action beyond conventional realms, extending directly into home, family and local community concerns, issues which trade unions in Britain have only just begun to take notice of. SEWA, as its name suggests, is also a collective organisation which mobilises women and successfully challenges the status quo, yet another challenge to the view of developing world women as passive and docile as we discussed in more detail in Chapter Three. The gender perspective on collective action which can be drawn out of this discussion is also salient to moving the debate forward. Drawing on White's (1992) account of women in rural Bangladesh, we discussed in Chapter Three the greater importance of social capital to women as compared to men in campaigning for their rights and improved conditions at home and at work. Links can be made here with Kapferer (1972) and Grieco (1996) and their recognition (albeit in different contexts) of the importance of social transactions and interactions to the mobilisation of support and collective action.

Secondly, SEWA is interesting in that it mobilises self-employed workers, individuals who would not normally come under the remit of trade union membership. In this, SEWA has charted territory which trade unions in the developed world have only just began to think of as serious new membership bases. Trade unions in Britain for example have woken up late to the need to improve representative democracy within their organisations and recognise the differing bargaining needs of under-represented groups such as women and workers from minority ethnic groups, who represent the majority of workers on nonstandard contracts (self-employed, part-time, temporary) (Labour Research, 1998; Cockburn, 1995; Cunnison and Stageman, 1995).

We also need to begin recognising that we need new models of what are considered appropriate bargaining arenas at work within the developing world context. With regard to the study of bargaining and campaigning by trade unions and other employee collectivities, we need to recognise that bargaining cannot just be studied only in terms of substantive issues and structures. What voiced accounts and in-depth ethnographic inquiry demonstrate is that bargaining is essentially about social interactions and power relationships. We still need to find much more about why and how people act in the way that they do, and how successful the choices that are made are, in terms of making real gains for members and for mobilising and maintaining membership support. Relating to the discussion above, there have been recent changes in strategies within the larger trade unions in Britain about the need for bargaining agendas to recognise the needs of under-represented groups (Dickens, 1997; Kirton and Healy, 1999). Unions have thus embarked upon numerous equality strategies designed to redress this (Greene and Kirton, 2000; Kirton and Greene, 2000a, 2000b).

Within the developing world context, such issues of representative democracy and equality are obviously relevant, however, we can also recognise other areas that should come under the bargaining remit of trade unions. One such example is that of child labour as was discussed in Chapter Three. The strategies of trade unions, employers and governments, need to recognise the social embeddedness of practices and processes and try to work with them to find new arenas of bargaining action.

Summary: Moving Towards Choice-making

What is missing from many accounts of trade union action at the local workplace level is the micro accounts of the how and why of collective action. In the developed world, collective organisations such as trade unions are struggling to maintain and mobilise membership in a time of economic flux, ideological individualism and government derision. The wider context is increasingly unfriendly to trade unions in general along with other social movements, and trade unions are attempting to find ways to renew themselves and make collective action a feasible and desirable response to the difficulties of working life. In the developing world context, similar factors challenge trade unions, but to a greater extent, where government oppression can take the most severest physical forms and where the penalties of loss of job have far greater consequences for the livelihood of those individuals concerned and their families. Additionally, it is in the developing world that perhaps we find the greatest need for groups which campaign for the rights of workers to humane levels of wages and conditions and where individuals have least power in the employment relationship as compared to their employers. Commentators can provide all kinds of possible avenues for trade union renewal or suggestion of more successful ways to mobilise and maintain collective support in the face of extreme obstacles. However, there is little consensus in this more macro theorising about what strategies might be most successful and more importantly for the construction of future strategies, why such strategies are successful. Research which aims to gain ethnographic detail and allows those involved to speak for themselves, so that we can come to greater understanding about the processes and interactions involved, is key to gaining some view about what strategies might be most successful in what particular contexts.

From the lock ethnographies, there was a clear suggestion from the workers and activists involved, that there should be maintenance of some conflict of interest, active resistance and public antagonism between the trade union and management. The important point however is that the terms of any cooperation with management at workplace level need to be carefully formulated if the support of members is to be maintained. It is not so much a question of whether to cooperate or not, but the terms of this cooperation. This ethnographic account has thus provided a useful insight into the way in which the employment relationship can be managed from the union activist/representative's point of view. Many writers agree that the employment relationship involves a dialectic of conflict and cooperation and this is clearly illustrated in employee perceptions at the lock companies also. However, in terms of the consequences of this for the behaviour of union leaders and managers, analysis often offers up dualistic models. For example, whether a union should be seen as moderate or militant, individualistic or collectivist, cooperative or adversarial, or a mixture, depending on the circumstances, and is concerned with outlining their relative benefits and disadvantages (Edwards, 1995; Kelly, 1996; Bacon and Storey, 1996). What ethnographic inquiry provides, in contrast, is a presentation of the way in which the people involved actually deal with this process of negotiation with management, and in so doing, offers more complex models of action linked to the particular context. In the developing world, where so many of those people involved remained unvoiced in the formal account, we need to build on such research methods to capture the informal processes and social interactions to better understand how workers may improve their working lives by working collectively.

Notes

1 Sections of this chapter have been published under Greene, A.M., Black, J. and Ackers, P. (2000), 'The Union Makes us Strong? A Study of the Dynamics of Workplace Union Leadership at Two Manufacturing Plants', *British Journal of Industrial Relations*, Vol. 38, 1, pp. 75–95 and Black, J., Greene, A.M. and Ackers, P. (1999), 'Clinging to Collectivism? Some Ethnographic Shopfloor Evidence from the British Lock Industry 1979–1998', *International Journal of Human Resource Management*, 10, 5, pp. 941–57.

2 Where membership of the recognised trade union is compulsory for employees.

3 Meeting with the LockCo convenor 22 January 1997.

4 Meeting held by the LockCo convenor on the shopfloor with one department and its shop stewards to discuss the pay settlement being offered 1 July 1997.

5 Meeting with the LockCo Convenor 9 October 1997.

Chapter Five

A Better Way: Authentic Voice, Authentic Participation in the Processes of Industrial Relations

We began this volume with the aim of demonstrating the utility and appropriateness of ethnographic methods to the study of industrial relations in the developing world. Throughout the course of the volume, we hope that we have brought alive the industrial relations of the lock companies, not only through our own ethnographic observations, but primarily through the voices of the workers, managers and trade unionists with whom we spent time: their comments, thoughts, stories, memories and behaviours. More importantly, we have linked such analysis to the developing world context, drawing out similar and different themes that have arisen and have pointed to the few texts that have used ethnographic methods within their research designs. We hope that we have been successful in demonstrating how illuminating such texts are, as compared to the conventional industrial relations accounts, in bringing to the fore, the voices of those involved. In this concluding chapter, we aim to summarise some of the key themes which we feel have emerged from the discussion, to point out some of the difficulties involved with ethnographic research and how these may be overcome in the developing world context, and finally, to suggest some fruitful areas for future industrial relations research.

Ethnographic Methods: the Importance of Capturing the Dramas

It is clear that ethnographic research allows a deeper understanding of the issues which frame the world-views of those involved in a particular research context. At the lock companies, and in our wider industrial relations research, we were interested in finding out what were the experiences and contexts that framed these views: in essence, seeing industrial relations as a series of social interactions rather than structures and issues. We wanted to explore why particular managerial change programmes failed or succeeded in different contexts. We were interested for example, in why initiatives which might be seen as positively empowering, in breaking down gender demarcations and ostensibly increasing gender equality, faced opposition from those workers they were supposed to help. As another example, why at such similar workplaces, did we find such different attitudes towards the trade union and such different levels of willingness to act collectively to support their trade union?

What became clear was that we could identify a variety of 'dramas', where employees had clear expectations about the roles that particular actors in the employment relationship should play. Dramaturgical analysis was useful as a way of exploring the importance of leadership and management styles in influencing perceptions of commitment and trust, the acceptance or rejection of workplace restructuring, and the maintenance and mobilisation of collective support. At the lock companies, we identified dramas based around managerial style (most notably paternalism), relations between workers (notably influenced by gender and family), and around negotiation and collective action. What also became clear as we became more deeply immersed within the workplace contexts was that what informed those expectations, and what became criteria for an 'appropriate part' in the 'appropriate' drama related to deeply embedded experiences and attitudes, some carried through many generations of family workers.

At both LockCo and KeyCo, the majority of employees had been employed at the company for more than 10 years. They thus had a long history of experience in the company from which to draw their views and opinions. In Chapter Two we discussed how opinions and views of management were set within a historical framework of traditional family paternalism. Their past experience saw a more personal and friendly employment relationship, where there was significant contact between managers and employees on the shopfloor, where managers worked their way up through the company from apprentice level, where there were joint decision-making and consultative committees, and where there was a large degree of company welfare involvement, both within the factory walls and in the wider Willenhall community. It was on the basis of these expectations that management were felt to fall short. In Chapter Three, we discussed how these world views were also framed and scripted within a context influenced by particular gendered work relations and by wider family and community influences.

In Chapter Four, we explored how the orientation of views towards the union was also placed within this frame of reference that reflects on their historical experience. For all of the reasons that workers condemned the company and managers, the union was praised. In some respects, the union had taken on some of the paternalistic involvement, which the companies had allowed to decline. A similar situation existed with regard to communication, contact and accessibility. The management was criticised for not making an effort to be more accessible and having more contact with the shopfloor. This was seen as a strength of the union at LockCo. The influence of the historical context of the workplace was thus clearly highlighted (Martin and Fryer, 1975; Fox, 1985, p. xii), where people's orientation and perceptions of the employment relationship were shaped by their past experiences and were related to an exchange relationship that rested on a framework of expectations of the terms of these relations.

Similar findings emerge from some of the voiced accounts, which we were able to find in the developing world context. Authors have used different language and terminology; Kapferer (1972) for example traces how the characters in his study deliberately manipulated social interactions for particular desired results. This involved the recognition of needing to present a certain image (we would say playing a certain part), where the frame of reference for such self-presentation relied on an awareness of wider community and family pressures and influences, and long embedded expectations. Similarly, Ramaswamy (1994), Wolf (1992) or White (1992) may not have talked specifically about dramas, but certainly present within their accounts are similar assertions about the need to present certain self images, and trace the way in which social action and interaction is influenced by prior experience and influences, some external to the workplace context.

Certainly, none of these conclusions are unique, or involve uncharted territory. However, they are certainly not the subject matter of most mainstream industrial relations accounts. Given the increased need to capture the informal and the difficulties experienced within the quantitative paradigm (as we discussed in Chapter One), that such relational areas become the subject matter of industrial relations research within the developing world context, becomes even more important.

We would now like to discuss some of the key areas, which we feel should form part of ethnographic industrial relations study:

1 the need for workplace level studies;
2 the need to introduce gender perspectives within industrial relations inquiry;
3 the need to extend industrial relations beyond the factory gates;
4 the need to study what industrial relations actors actually do;
5 the need to break away from the binarism between the developed and the developing world.

The Need for Workplace Level Studies

This volume has highlighted the benefits of workplace level studies that build up a detailed picture of surrounding contextual factors. It has focused on the influence of the specific local workplace context, on workers' perceptions of their work lives and their attachments to social groups. Our lock research highlights the diversity of views and attitudes across very similar workplaces in very similar contexts, and lends supports to doubts about relying solely on findings drawn from large-scale surveys at national level. The specific differences in organisation, structure and policies within different workplaces can be important influences on perceptions and attitudes across similar contexts. To get an in-depth picture of the nature of commitment and identities surrounding the employment relationship, qualitative case studies at workplace level are extremely valuable. When dealing with complex socio-psychological attachments and relationships, it is not enough to rely on a short survey answer.

The Need to Introduce Gender Perspectives within Industrial Relations Inquiry

Chapter Three offered a critique of the neglect of gender perspectives within conventional Western industrial relations accounts. Given that those who remain unvoiced within the formal industrial relations account form an even larger group, it is not surprising that Wolf (1992, p. 9) states that Third World women remain 'faceless and voiceless' in most studies. This is a significant gap, given that just as in the developed world, women play a major role in the family economy, and often the woman is the primary breadwinner in the family (Grieco et al., 1996; Kasturi et al., 1990). We contend that this gap needs to be filled, and given the lower power positions and lack of formal power roles, which women hold in the employment relationship, we are unlikely to be able to fill this gap using conventional research methods within quantitative paradigms. Ethnographic methods are key to capturing informal processes and interactions and ethnographic inquiry will often force the researcher to take notice of gender issues and look at the different experiences of both women and men, rather than looking at workers for example, as homogenous.

However, we also discuss that ethnographers can be as gender blind as other researchers, and in Chapter Three we discuss a number of ethnographically-informed accounts which have not taken gender issues on board. Indeed the lock studies themselves did not begin from an agenda in which gender issues were an expected subject matter, however, as the research project progressed, there was a quick realisation that gender issues were very pertinent to the discussion. Our contention, after emerging from the research process and surveying the field, is that industrial relations studies should always try and consider gender perspectives within the analysis, because one of the core subjects (and we would state that such a concern needs to be prioritised) of industrial relations is concerned with social interactions, people interacting within the employment relationship/s. Industrial relations is concerned with women and men and thus gender perspectives will always be a salient area of inquiry.

This is important in both the developed and the developing world in terms of challenging stereotypes about what men and women can and should do, and how they can and should interact, in work situations. In Chapter Three there was discussion of the number of ways in which ethnographically based study demonstrated the inappropriateness of various gender stereotypes, or offered contextualised explanations for where such stereotypes were upheld.

The Need to Extend Industrial Relations beyond the Factory Gates

A need to look beyond the workplace context connects closely with the need to integrate gender within industrial relations studies. In Chapter Three, a critique was offered regarding the neglect of family and community issues within industrial relations. What was reiterated again and again, not only through our own lock studies, but also through many of the other research texts that we have referred to throughout this volume, was that industrial relations should not just be concerned with what goes on inside the office or factory. Industrial relations analyses must consider the influences of wider families and communities. Within the lock studies, what framed what were seen as appropriate parts in the appropriate dramas, included not only current workplace experience, but family situations, the influence of wider kinship experience, concerns for physical community context, and collective family memory (Grieco, 1996) handed down through generations of family members. The importance of these influences outside of the workplace were also clear in all of the developing world voiced accounts which we came across. Ackers' (1999) communitarian view of industrial relations, with its concern to include family and community perspectives within industrial relations analyses will provide a useful model for future research.

The Need to Study what Industrial Relations Actors Actually Do

We did not focus on managerial action within the lock ethnographies. However, trade unions and trade union action are core subject matters for conventional industrial relations and formed a major part of our studies at the lock companies. Ethnographically-informed accounts begin to fill a gap in the field (see discussion in Chapter Four), notably looking in depth at how and why trade union leaders and members do what they do. Ethnography allows a view of action in situ, placing social action and interaction within its context. In a worldwide climate which is generally unfavourable to trade unions and other collective support movements, initiatives to recruit, mobilise and maintain membership support will be helpfully informed by the valuable in depth analysis that ethnography offers.

This volume also presents how in common with other industrial relations actors, trade union leaders and members must also play their appropriate parts in the dramas of the employment relationship. An important facet of the mobilisation and maintenance process for trade unionists, is being aware of the context in which they are acting and interacting: finding the appropriate role is a complex task.

The Need to Break Away from the Binarism between the Developed and the Developing World

Finally, a common theme flowing through this volume has been the need to move away from analyses that maintain rigid binarisms between the developing and the developed world, traditional and modern, new and old. The chapters of this volume are filled with instances where, by constantly looking across and making comparisons between the developing and the developed we begin to understand that this binarism is not useful. It is not that we can find some 'lost world' of industrial relations in the developing world context or that the developed should be seen as the model of modernity. There are numerous occasions in this volume where the traditional and the modern are found together in particular contexts, where both developed and developing world contexts see industrial relations actors trying to manage the past as well as the present, and where both have lessons to offer for each other. This is especially the case, given the level of the globalised economy, which we discuss in greater detail later in this chapter.

Such lessons may also emerge from the differences (as well as similarities) that are found between national employment systems or the way in which workplace industrial relations are affected by both local community as well as wider national contexts. Industrial relations as a discipline remains ethnocentric, with research primarily based in Britain, North America and Australia (Ackers, 1999; Whitfield and Strauss, 1998). Even where industrial relations in other parts of the world are the subject of study, the analysis is usually based around what other countries can learn from the European, American or Australian example. As an example, Fosh's (1997) article explores whether the experience of British trade unions offers any lessons for the trade union movement in Hong Kong. We would suggest that as useful a route of inquiry might be whether the Hong Kong trade union movement offers any lessons for that in Britain. This direction of inquiry is not the conventional choice. Industrial relations as a discipline, must move its sights beyond Western models and research subjects and become more polycentric in outlook. In Chapter Three for example, we discussed the issue of child labour and suggested in Chapter Four that this should be seen as a collective bargaining issue in contexts where it is relevant. The experience of trade union movements in the developing world, has in some cases been far more forward thinking and proactive in its strategies for renewal and renaissance than that in the developed, as the example of SEWA in Chapter Three illustrates.

Ethnographic Methods: Some Pitfalls and Some Suggestions

It appears useful at this point in the discussion to add some note of caution into our analysis. We are not advocating that all industrial relations studies should be ethnographically based, and we recognise the important findings and theorising which have emerged from quantitative studies, particularly some of the large scale surveys (see Marginson, 1998 for a summary). However, what we hope that this volume has demonstrated, is that there is a significant lack of ethnographically-based accounts within mainstream industrial relations in both the developed and the developing world, and that this lack has significant consequences for the types of knowledge and understandings that are gained. What is important is that there is more balance in the field, and that there are the voiced and ethnographically detailed accounts to complement, support and challenge those emerging from more conventional research.

It should be noted that ethnography can not be seen as a panacea, and that ethnography is not without its own problems and weaknesses. Ethnography is certainly not an easy research option: the level of immersion in the research site required over a long period of time plus the demands of constantly observing, writing notes and talking to people, is a considerable intellectual effort.

Who should attempt to extend the field of industrial relations into the developing world context; should it be researchers from the same national or local culture or should Westerners attempt industrial relations ethnographies in the developing world context? Our feeling is that both groups should and indeed this volume has discussed both types of research. However it should be recognised that the research effort becomes increasingly more difficult when ethnographic study is engaged with, in a context where there are great differences between researcher and researched and given the emphasis on voice and discourse within ethnography, where a different language is spoken. Ethnography relies on the researcher being able to immerse themselves in the research context and fears of not being accepted by those one is trying to research is a constant problem. Looking at researchers' own accounts of their research process is extremely useful in this regard and indicates that, while difficult, the task is not impossible. Maren Bell (Srinivas et al., 1979) speaks of her difficulties as a West German woman researching an industrial slum in Karipur, India: 'I was an unmarried foreign girl and the people who came into contact with me had great difficulty placing me socially and in understanding me' (ibid., p. 141). Maren Bell had to make the effort to gain the necessary language skills, stayed with a local family for a lengthy period of time and was accompanied by a trusted member of the local community during her research project. Such efforts obviously require a long period of time. Exactly similar situations were experienced by Diane Lauren Wolf (1992) in Java or Sarah White (1992) in Bangladesh. In other words, ethnography is not easy, but the difficulties are not insurmountable.

Anthropological ethnography has usually involved the outsider researching the native in a context alien to their own (Prasad and Prasad, 2000). Ethnography within industrial relations and Organisation Studies has developed this anthropological ethnography so that the fieldworker enters an 'alien' organisational culture to study the 'natives', even though researcher and researched may share the same national culture (ibid.). However, it is not even that being 'native' or 'going native' is necessarily the solution, certainly this holds its own set of pitfalls. Prasad and Prasad (ibid.) provide a useful summary of the dangers which can beset someone researching their own culture and the way in which such research is often criticised by the academic college. Such criticisms often revolve around the difficulty in maintaining distance between the researcher and the researched. There is a case to be made for the need to maintain some objectivity and distance between the researcher and the researched: too much subjectivity has been seen as a weakness of some ethnographic research. Ethnographic work has been criticised for being flawed by partial perspectives, what is called '*over-rapport*', where the views of the researched are taken over without question. Hammersley and Atkinson (1983, p. 98) specifically mention Paul Willis' *Learning to Labour* (1977) in these terms, where the book becomes a celebration of the lads involved rather than an objective analysis of their views in context. However, it is equally problematic to believe that the researcher can be completely objective or detached.

Overall, as researchers, we have to be aware of the authenticity of the ethnographic account. The need to be reflexive about the research project, as discussed in Chapter One is key here. All of the foreign researchers above were very aware that the place of a foreigner as a researcher meant that there were particular problems which had to be overcome as best one could in order to gain the most authentic account. Similarly, 'native' researchers also need to recognise their part in the research process. The researcher has to be reflexive about their own involvement in the research, something not often considered in other research paradigms. The emphasis on the need to hear the voices of those researched is important, so the interpretations made by the researcher are seen as informed by the voiced account, rather than by their own opinions. The primary objective is to acquire the most authentic account as possible from the people that we speak to, observe and interact with, within the constraints and circumstances of the particular research context.

We are also not advocating any purist form of ethnography as was discussed in Chapter One. Morgan and Smircich (1980) point to the importance of not 'pigeonholing' techniques to fit with designated epistemological views. Any given technique can lend itself to a variety of uses according to the orientation of the researcher. Regarding ethnography specifically (but which we feel can be applied to many research projects, using different methods) Geertz (1973, p. 6) points out that:

> From one point of view, doing ethnography is establishing rapport, selecting informants, transcribing texts, taking genealogies, mapping fields, keeping a diary, and so on. But it is not these things, techniques, and received procedures that define the enterprise. What defines it is the kind of intellectual effort it is.

Part of that framework of reflexivity is that the virtues of techniques and methods used must be seen within the context of the assumptions on which the researcher acts. Concentrating on methods obscures the link between the assumptions that the researcher holds and the research effort, which gives the *illusion* that it is methods, rather than the orientation of the researcher that generates particular forms of knowledge (Morgan and Smircich, 1980, p. 499). So, an assessment of any research should look more at the thinking behind it than the actual methods used. What is missing from industrial relations currently, and which would be of particular use in developing world contexts is research that attempts to uncover the picture of the social world investigated in terms of the views of those involved, with every effort made to present their own views and allow their voices to be heard.

Some Future Research Agendas

So far, we have summarised our view of the importance and value of ethnography to industrial relations, and suggested some of the areas of concern that arose while researching in the lock companies and while writing this volume. We would also like to suggest some areas which may provide fruitful and interesting new areas of research within the industrial relations arena and which would benefit from ethnographic inquiry.

Breaking Down the Binarism: Globalised Companies

That we live and work in a highly globalised economy has particular significance for industrial relations. What is clear is that industrial relations crosses international borders, and that this means that there is even more utility in attempting to break down the rigid binarism that exists between developing and developed world. To reiterate the discussion in Chapter One, we should not think that what happens in the developing world has little relevance for greater understanding of what is happening in the developed and vice versa. As Macdonald (1997) summarises, globalisation has disturbed traditional industrial relations arrangements in a number of ways. Firstly, the boundaries of the market place have been expanded so that multinational companies have created very complex international production networks. Secondly, globalisation has disturbed the status quo between capital and labour as capital becomes more mobile in an one international environment, while the potentialities of new information technologies open up considerable inter-enterprise networks. Do we for instance, need to call into question the traditional boundaries of the enterprise? Thirdly, there are contradictory forces at work within globalisation, on the one hand convergence of industrial relations systems and practices is being fostered by these global enterprise networks, while on the other hand, there is clear evidence of increasing resistance to convergence and evidence of increasing diversity of practices (Hyman, 1999). We need to think about how our research methods might most usefully investigate the impact of such developments, and the value that ethnographic inquiry might offer.

With specific reference to the British lock companies that we researched, the purchase of a factory in China in 1996 has had and will have, significant consequences for industrial relations at the lock companies and in the lock communities and is an area that we would like to further investigate in the future. Firstly, the factory in China employs almost as many people as there are in the entire British lock industry. While the purchase was in its early stages during the period of research fieldwork and therefore was not a key topic of discussion, already, some employees had commented that they felt that the existence of this factory was a very real threat to their jobs, and therefore to their local community, reliant as it was on the lock industry. From the trade union officials and representatives, there were initial concerns about the detrimental effects of having employees of the same company working under such different conditions on a global scale. Certainly, the union leaders were concerned that the Chinese workers were not unionised and that (as was discussed in Chapter Four) the political and economic climate in China was so unfavourable to trade unionism. These are obviously issues that many multinational companies face and which would provide fruitful areas for future research inquiry. It would be of great value to be able to undertake an ethnographically informed research project within the Chinese factory to complement that in the British, to aid understanding about what the experiences of the lock workers are within different contexts: can we, for example, talk about a global occupational community of lock workers?

The Impact of New Information Technologies (ICTs) on Industrial Relations

There are many different facets of the discussion regarding ICTs and industrial relations that we could engage with, ranging from the scope that they have for flexibility in production processes, to the emergence of virtual teams (Macdonald, 1997). Given some of the core themes emerging from our lock studies, in particular the challenges which trade unions and other collectivist social movements face in mobilising and maintaining membership support, we would like to offer up the possibility of researching the potentiality of new ICTs in this area in particular. In discussing whether we need to question the traditional boundaries of the enterprise or workplace, this also links into questions about global communities of workers and therefore global trade unions and globalised collective action. Such a research topic has the added advantages of bringing up many of the areas that we have suggested need further addressing in mainstream industrial relations, in particular the participation of women in industrial relations and the activities and social interactions of trade union activists.

Currently, the academic industrial relations literature has been slow to reflect or deliberate upon the organising opportunities that new ICTs offer the trade union and other social movements, with some notable exceptions (Castells, 1991; Lee, 1997; Pliskin et al., 1997; Shostak, 1999). Greene et al. (2000: http://www.geocities.com/unionsonline, http://www.e-collectivism.org.uk) offer a summary of such benefits and opportunities. For example, helping to increase the participation of those who are most time poor, notably women and those on non standard employment contracts, and thus increase membership and maintenance of that membership support.

Globalisation has led to an increased dispersal of employees over a wider area, which makes it more difficult for trade unions and other support movements to recruit, represent and mobilise using traditional methods. New ICTS and electronic forms of organising can provide features of close-knit community relationships over a much more dispersed organisational base. Additionally, there are resource issues to consider; achieving close physical proximity of union representatives to members is very expensive. New ICTs change recruitment frontiers because they enable organisation on the basis of informal resources, which is less expensive to organise. It would be interesting for example to explore how the lock workers' trade union might be able to engage in the representation and mobilisation of the Chinese lock workers, across international boundaries using the technology available.

One of the established prerequisites of the union renewal thesis (Fairbrother, 1989) involves the need for union structures and leadership to be more accountable and more representative. This is in order to avoid accommodation with management, separation from members, routinisation of methods and conservatism of aims (Gall, 1999). Such issues also came out clearly as aspects of the 'part' that union leaders at the lock companies were expected to play in the dramas of negotiation and collective action. The proximity of union members to local, regional, national and international on-line trade union resources, through ICTs, increases the transparency of the behaviour of union officials to the union membership and enables an independent assessment of the performance of officials, in a manner that was never previously possible. 'Cyber-unionism' thus has the potential to alter the bargaining positions of ordinary union members in respect of union leadership. Such opportunities would obviously also apply to other social movements requiring participant support and mobilisation of collective action.

New ICTs also provide opportunities for enhanced forms of solidarity and communication (Trench and O'Donnell, 1997). Reviewing the Internet experience of ordinary union members in the USA, Shostak (1999) indicates the importance of the new proximity of rank and file members to official union resources offered by ICTs. The old understanding of physical proximity as a primary precondition for solidarity (Greene et al., 2000) is clearly under challenge; virtual organisation is a new and important key in the process of synchronisation of political and industrial movements (Pliskin et al., 1997). In support of the suggestion that global collective action can be encouraged, new ICTs also make it less important to work on a permanent membership basis for many levels of solidarity actions – ties can be restored at any point through listings and social networks. The recent anti-World Bank activities have used affinity structures, meaning that groups who have internal links can provide support for one another or are able to link into hub activities through the net and welcome facilities at websites.

It is also important to recognise the obstacles which users of the new ICTs face. In practice, the use of new technology in any extended way has been limited to those unions organising in sectors that are computer literate and which are predominantly white collar. In addition, it is obvious that the use of the Internet and of new ICTs has largely been confined to the richer countries of the developed world. Effective utilisation of new ICTs obviously requires unions and other organisations to consider the wider context of their membership and how ICT use can be encouraged in the lower-paid sectors of the economy. In particular, one British trade union, Unison, is exceptional in actively encouraging its membership to participate in web activity by offering free Internet services. Given the diversity of access to ICTs across the world and within national contexts, this is an initiative which clearly has the potential to make electronic forms more socially inclusive, but which has not been taken up by many other unions, particularly those with predominantly blue collar membership, where perhaps the need is most acute. While usage of ICTs are restricted to particular parts of the world economy, there is no doubt that their use is spreading extremely fast, and despite all the obstacles, ICTs are being put to use in projects all over the developing world with great success (see www.geocities.com/transport_and_society and http://www.teledemocracy.org/).

Such a discussion could obviously continue in more depth, and there is an almost endless list of possibilities and obstacles that could be engaged with. However, such a discussion is beyond the remit of this book. What we have attempted to demonstrate here, is that there are new and exciting areas of industrial relations research to emerge from the globalised economy and which relate clearly to some of the themes which have emerged from our own ethnographic inquiry. A quantitative survey of the use of ICTs is not enough to allow us to understand the processes of social interaction being engaged with, or to advance knowledge about their implications for industrial relations in the future. Research within an ethnographic paradigm would be of great value in attempting to explore why and how people engage with the new ICTs and what place in the dramas of the employment relationship such social interaction plays.

Epilogue

And so we come to the end of our journey. The existing phase of the research project at the lock companies is over, and one of the most difficult things about ethnographic research is 'letting go' of the project. We obviously had to establish a cut off point and decide that from a certain point in time, we had to stop tracking the dynamics and processes of industrial relations. This was difficult, because it is obvious that life continues at the lock companies and the dynamics of the employment relationship are constantly changing, being recreated and reconstructed. It is obvious that if we entered the companies now, some of the findings will need to be amended. We have also recognised through our analysis that there are new areas emerging, which would be interesting to research: in particular issues regarding the Chinese factory, globalised lock community and use of new technologies. However, this is always an issue with research of any kind. It is reassuring to recognise, that however small the field is presently, there are people carrying out ethnographically-informed industrial relations studies in many different parts of the world. Our aspiration is that such interest will increase and industrial relations as a discipline will be challenged and complemented by the rich array of voiced accounts, which may emerge in the future.

APPENDIX

Ethnographic Resource Archive

This archive is intended to provide a helpful resource, outlining details of some of the ethnographic studies that have been discussed within this volume, from both the developed and developing world. The archive offers the source of the text which can be cross referenced with the bibliography, and summarises details regarding the context in which the research was carried out, the methods employed and the themes to emerge from the research. Such an archive highlights the richness of the lock ethnographies in terms of emerging themes and indicates where similar themes arise in the other ethnographic studies.

Source text	Research context	Research methodology	Emergent themes
Greene, A.M. (1999)	Comparative study of two companies in the West Midlands lock industry, England. Research at LockCo covered the period 1983–98.	1 Ethnographic observation, including attendance at meetings. 2 Archive of interviews at LockCo 1983–98 with 95 employees, 38 union representatives and 39 managers. 3 Archive of interviews at KeyCo 1996 with 20 employees 2 union representatives and 9 managers. 4 Diary kept by LockCo union convenor.	1 Social relations of industrial relations. 2 Expected dramas of paternalism, gendered relations and collective action and negotiation. 3 Link between workplace relations and family and community influences.
Ramaswamy, E.A. (1994)	Study of one rayon spinning factory and the outlying community over a 15 year period from 1977.	1 Ethnographic observation. 2 Historical and archival research. 3 Interviews and informal meetings with union representatives, managers and employees. 4 Talking to employees outside of the workplace setting.	1 Focus on the social interactions of industrial relations. 2 Dramas of paternalism. 3 Link between workplace relations and family and community influences.

Source text	Research methodology	Research context	Emergent themes
Kapferer (1972)	Study of a Zambian textile factory and surrounding community over a year period, looking specifically at two industrial action events.	1 Ethnographic observation over a 6 month period inside the factory. 2 Interviews and informal meetings with union representatives, managers and employees. 3 Talking to employees outside of the workplace setting. Year long fieldwork research living in the local Bisa community.	1 Focus on the social interactions of industrial relations. 2 Link between workplace relations and family and community influences. 3 Dramas of collective action.
Grieco et al. (1996)	Study of male and female porters in Accra, Ghana and their transport use 1993–95. Is a transport studies research project but has valuable and insightful accounts of industrial relations processes.	1 Ethnographic observation of the porters at work. 2 Interviews and informal meetings with male and female porters and their families. 3 Involved 1013 respondents.	1 Focus on the social interactions of industrial relations. 2 Link between relations at work and family and community influences. 3 Dramas of gendered relations 4 Challenge gender stereotypes. 5 Offers voiced biographies of particular workers. 6 Child labour issues.

Source text	Research context	Research methodology	Emergent themes
Grieco (1996)	Study of communities in London, England's East end and their labour migration to hoping communities of East Anglia.	1 Historical study using diaries and other documentation. 2 Interviews and informal meetings with community members.	1 Focus on the social interactions of industrial relations. 2 Link between relations at work and family and community influences. 3 Dramas of gendered relations. 4 Dramas of collective memory.
Wolf (1992)	Study of women factory workers in rural Java over a 5 year period.	1 Ethnographic observation: the research included living amongst the villagers for a year, living in a women's factory dormitory for a month, when the researcher kept detailed observation notes. 2 Visits to 12 factories. 3 Diaries kept by women factory workers. 4 Interviews and informal meetings with women workers and their families. 5 Survey data involving 250 households.	1 Focus on the social interactions of industrial relations. 2 Link between relations at work and family and community influences. 3 Dramas of gendered relations. 4 Offers voiced biographies of particular workers.

Source text	Research context	Research methodology	Emergent themes
Kramsjo and Wood (1992)	8 case studies of Proshika, self help collective organisations over a 3 month period in 1986 in Bangladesh.	1 Ethnographic observation at Proshika campaigns and events. 2 Interviews and informal meetings with group leaders and group followers.	1 Focus on the social interactions of industrial relations. 2 Link between relations at work and family and community influences. 3 Dramas of collective action. 4 Challenge gender stereotypes. 5 Offers voiced biographies of particular activists.
Margold (1999)	Case study of women workers within an electronics factory in the Philippines, and focuses particularly on their struggle for political voice.	1 Ethnographic observation. 2 Interviews and informal meetings with women workers and union activists. 3 Historical analysis. 4 Individual chronicles of women involved.	1 Focus on the social interactions of industrial relations: in particular collective action. 2 Link between relations at work and family and community influence. 3 Dramas of collective action. 4 Challenge gender stereotypes. 5 Offers voiced biographies of particular workers.

Source text	Research context	Research methodology	Emergent themes
White (1992)	Study of women in rural villages in Bangladesh.	1 Ethnographic observation. 2 Researcher lived within a village for 10 months in 1985–86, followed by numerous visits until 1990. 3 Detailed case studies of 30 households. 4 Interviews and informal meetings with women and their families. 5 Individual chronicles of women involved.	1 Link between relations at work and family and community influence. 2 Challenge gender stereotypes. 3 Dramas of gendered relations. 4 Offers voiced biographies of particular women.

Bibliography

Abbeglen, J. (1958), *The Japanese Factory: Aspects of its social organisation*, Glencoe: Free Press.

Ackers, P. (1988), 'Changes in Workplace Industrial Relations in the West Midlands Manufacturing Industry in the 1980s', MPhil thesis, University of Wolverhampton.

Ackers, P. (1998), 'Review Essay: On Paternalism: Seven Observations on the Uses and Abuses of the Concept in Industrial Relations, Past and Present', *Historical Studies in Industrial Relations*, Vol. 5, pp. 173–93.

Ackers, P. (1999), 'Industrial Relations and the Spirit of Community', *Loughborough University Research Series*, 15.

Ackers, P. and Black, J. (1991), 'Paternalistic capitalism: An Organisation Culture in Transition', in M. Cross and G. Payne (eds), *Work and the Enterprise Culture*, Falmer Press.

Ackers, P. and Black, J. (1992), 'Managing Organised Labour: A Tale of Two Companies', *Journal of Industrial Affairs*, Vol. 2.

Ackers, P. and Payne, J. (1998), 'Trade Unions and Social Partnership: Rhetoric, reality, strategy', *International Journal of Human Resource Management*, Vol. 9, 3, pp. 529–50.

Ackers, P., Smith, C. and Smith, P. (1996), *The New Work Place and Trade Unionism*, London and New York: Routledge.

Adams, R. (1959), 'On the Relations between Plantation and Creole Cultures', in *Plantation Systems of the New World: Papers and discussion summaries of the seminar on plantation systems of the new world*, San Juan, Puerto Rico, Washington: Pan American Press.

Alexander, R. (1962), 'Brazil, Argentina and Chile', in Walter Galenson (ed.), *Labor in Developing Economies*, Berkeley: University of California Press, pp. 138–86.

Anker, R. (1997), 'Theories of Occupational Segregation by Sex: An overview', *International Labour Review*, Vol. 36, 7, pp. 315–40.

Bacon, N. and Storey, J. (1996), 'Individualism and Collectivism and the Changing Role of Trade Unions', in P. Ackers, C. Smith and P. Smith (eds), *The New Work Place and Trade Unionism*, London: Routledge, pp. 41–76.

Bannerjee, N. (1985), *Women Workers in the Unorganised Sector*, Hydrabad: Sangam Books.

Bardhan, P. (ed.) (1989), *Conversations between Economists and Anthropologists: Methodological issues in measuring economic change in rural India*, Delhi: Oxford University Press.

Barker, J. and Downing, H. (1980), 'Word Processing and the Transformation of the Patriarchal Relations of Control in the Office', *Capital and Class*, Spring, 10, pp. 65–99.

Barling, J., Fullagar, C. and Kelloway, E.K. (1992), *The Union and its Members: A psychological approach*, New York: Oxford University Press.

Batstone, E., Boraston, I. and Frenkel, S. (1977), *Shop Stewards in Action: The organisation of work place conflict and accommodation*, Oxford: Basil Blackwell.

Beardsley, R., Hall, K. and Ward, R. (1959), *Village Japan*, University of Chicago Press.

Beechey, V. (1980), *Unequal Work*, London: Verso.

Bello, W. and Rosenfeld, S. (1990), 'The Making of an Insurrectionary Working Class', in W. Bello and S. Rosenfeld (eds), *Dragons in Distress, Asia's Miracle Economies in Crisis*, Harmondswoth: Penguin, ch. 1.

Bennett, J.W. and Ishino, I. (1963), *Paternalism in the Japanese Economy: Anthropological Studies of Oyaburn-Kobun patterns*, Minneapolis: University of Minnesota.

Bennett, J.W. (1968), 'Paternalism', in D.L. Sill (ed.), *Encyclopedia of the Social Sciences*, Vol. 11, USA: Macmillan/Free Press, pp. 472–77.

Berger P.L. and Luckman, T. (1979), *The Social Construction of Reality*, Harmondsworth: Penguin.

Black, J. and McCabe, D. (1998), 'Jointism and the Role of the Workplace Union in the Auto-Components Industry', *New Technology, Work and Employment*, Vol. 13, 1, pp. 39–48.

Black, J. and Neathey, F. (1989), 'Labour and Deskilling: A critique of managerial control in the glass industry', in W. Chua (ed.), *Critical Perspectives in Management Control*, London: Lowe and Puxty, pp. 161–87.

Black, J., Greene, A.M. and Ackers, P. (1997), 'Size and Effectiveness: A case study of a small Uunion', *Industrial Relations Journal*, June, 28, 2, pp. 135–49.

Black, J., Greene, A.M. and Ackers, P. (1999), 'Clinging to Collectivism? Some Ethnographic Shopfloor Evidence from the British Lock Industry 1979–1998', *International Journal of Human Resource Management*, Vol. 10, 5, pp. 941–57.

Blyton, P. and Turnbull, P. (1998), *The Dynamics of Employee Relations*, London: Macmillan.

Brissett, D. and Edgley, C. (1990), 'The Dramaturgical Perspective', in D. Brissett and C. Edgely (eds), *Life as Theater: A dramaturgical sourcebook*, New York: Aldine de Gruyter.

Brown, E. and Wright, M. (1994), 'The Empirical Tradition in Workplace Bargaining Tesearch', *British Journal of Industrial Relations*, Vol. 32, pp. 153–64.

Burawoy, M. (1974), 'Constraint and Manipulation in Industrial Conflict: A comparison of strikes among Zambian workers in a clothing factory and the mining industry', *Institute of African Studies*, Communication 10, University of Zambia.

Burawoy, M. (1979), *Manufacturing Consent: Changes in the labour process under monopoly capitalism*, University of Chicago Press.

Castells, M. (1991), *The Information City: Information technology, economic restructuring and the urban-regional process*, Oxford: Blackwell.

Cavendish, R. (1982), *Women on the Line*, London: Routledge and Kegan Paul.

Chandrasekhar, C. (1997), 'The Economic Consequences of the Abolition of Child Labour: An Indian case study', *Journal of Political Science*, Vol. 24, 3, pp. 157–79.

Clegg, H.A. (1979), *The Changing System of Industrial Relations in Great Britain*, Oxford: Blackwell.

Cockburn, C. (1989), 'Equal Opportunities: The long and short agenda', *Industrial Relations Journal*, Autumn, pp. 213–225

Cockburn, C. (1991), *In the Way of Women*, Basingstoke: Macmillan.

Cockburn, C. (1995), *Strategies for Gender Democracy*, Brussels: European Commission.

Cohen, S. and Fosh, P. (1988), '"You Are the Trade Union", Studies for Trade Unionists', *Workers Educational Association*, Vol. 14, 53.

Coleman, J.S. (1990), *Foundations of Social Theory*, Harvard University Press.

Coleman, J.S. (1988), 'Social Capital in the Creation of Human Capital', *American Journal of Sociology*, Vol. 94, pp. 95–120.

Collinson, D. (1994), 'Strategies of Resistance: Power, knowledge and subjectivity in the workplace', in J. Jermier et al (eds), *Resistance and Power in Organisations*, London: Routledge, pp. 25–69.

Collinson, D. and Collinson, M. (1989), 'Sexuality in the Workplace: The domination of men's sexuality', in J. Hearn et al. (eds), *The Sexuality of Organisation*, London: Sage, pp. 86–108.

Cully, M., Woodland, S., O'Reilly, A. and Dix, G. (1999), *Britain at Work*, London: Routledge.

Cunnison, S. and Stageman, J. (1995), *Feminising the Unions*, Aldershot: Avebury.

Curtis, D. (1994), 'Owning without Owners, Managing with Few Managers: Lessons from Third World irrigation', in S. Wright, *Anthropology of Organisations*, Routledge, pp. 56–68.

Curtis, K. (1999), 'Bottom-Up: Poverty and welfare poverty discourse: ethnography to the rescue?', *Urban Anthropology and Studies of Cultural Systems and World Economic Development*, 28, 2.

Czarniawska-Jeorges, Barbara (1992), *Exploring Complex Organisations*, London: Sage Publications.

Czarniawrska-Jeorges, Barbara (1997), *Narrating the Organisation*, University of Chicago Press.

Darlington, R. (1994), *The Dynamics of Work Place Unionism: Shop Stewards' Organisation in Three Merseyside Plants*, London: Mansell.

Delbridge, R. (1998), *Life on the Line in Contemporary Manufacturing*, Oxford University Press.

Department of Trade and Industry (DTI) (1996), 'Competitive Analysis of the Lock Industry in the UK', Keynote Ltd.

Dickens, L. (1997), 'Gender, Race and Employment Equality in Britain: Inadequate strategies and the role of industrial relations actors', *Industrial Relations Journal*, Vol. 28, 4, pp. 282–9.

Drummond, D.K. (1995), *Crewe: Railway town, company and people 1840–1914*, Aldershot: Scholar Press.

Edwards, C. and Heery, E. (1985), 'The Incorporation of Workplace Trade Unionism: Some Evidence from the Mining Industry', *Sociology*, Vol. 19, pp. 345–63.

Edwards, P. (1995), 'From Industrial Relations to the Employment Relationship', *Relations Industrielles*, Vol. 50, 1, pp. 39–63.

Edwards, P.K. (ed.), (1995), *Industrial Relations: Theory and Practice in Britain*, Oxford: Blackwell.

Fairbrother, P. (1989), 'Work Place Unionism in the 1980s: A process of renewal?', *Workers' Educational Association*, Studies for Trade Unionists, Vol. 15, 57.

Fetterman, D.M. (1989), *Ethnography: Step by step*, Applied Social Research Methods Series, Sage Publications, Vol. 17.

Ford, T. (1953), *Man and the Land in Peru*, Gainesville: University of Florida Press.

Fosh, P. (1993), 'Membership Participation and Work Place Trade Unionism: The possibility of renewal', *British Journal of Industrial Relations*, December, pp. 577–92.

Fosh, P. (1997), 'The Future for Hong Kong Trade Unions: What they can learn from the British trade unions' experience of adversity 1979–1997?', *Employee Relations*, Vol. 19, 5, pp. 466–95.

Fox, A. (1985), *History and Heritage: The Social origins of the British Industrial Relations System*, London: Allen and Unwin.

Friedman, R.A. and McDaniel, D.C. (1998), 'In the Eye of the Beholder: Ethnography in the study of work', in K. Whitfield and G. Strauss (eds) (1998), *Researching the World of Work: Strategies and methods in studying industrial relations*, Cornell University Press, pp. 113–127.

Gabriel, Y. (2000), *Storytelling in organizations*, Oxford University Press.

Gall, G. (1999), 'The Prospects for Workplace Trade Unionism: Evaluating Fairbrother's union renewal thesis', *Capital and Class*, Vol. 66, pp. 149–57.

Gardner, W. and Avolio, B. (1998), 'The charismatic relationship: A dramaturgical perspective', *Academy of Management Review*, Vol. 23, 1, pp. 32–59.

Geertz, C. (1965), *The Social History of an Indonesian Town*, Cambridge, Mass.: MIT Press.

Geertz, C. (1973), *The Interpretation of Cultures: Selected Essays*, New York: Fontana Press.

Giddens, A. (1991), *The Consequences of Modernity*, Part I, Cambridge: Polity Press.

Goffman, E. (1959), *The Presentation of the Self in Everyday Life*, Harmondsworth: Penguin.

Goldthorpe, J.H., Lockwood, J., Bechhofer, F. and Platt, J. (1968), *The Affluent Worker: Industrial attitudes and behaviour*, London: Cambridge University Press.

Grace, E. (1990), *Short-circuiting Labour: Unionising electronic workers in Malaysia*, Selangor: Institute of Social Analysis.

Grant, D. (1996), 'Metaphors, Human Resource Management and Control', in C. Oswick and D. Grant (eds), *Organisation Development: Metaphorical explorations*, London: Pitman, pp. 193–207.

Green, P. (1989), 'Women and Work in the Black Country: Locked into a sexual division of labour?', unpublished MA thesis, University of Wolverhampton.

Greene, A.M. (1999), 'Employees, Managers and the Trade Union: Changes and continuities in the employment relationship 1983–1998. A Study in the West Midlands Lock Industry', unpublished PhD thesis, University of Wolverhampton.

Greene, A.M. (forthcoming), 'Industrial Relations and Women', in P. Ackers and A. Wilkinson (eds), *Reworking Industrial Relations: New perspectives on employment and society*, Oxford University Press.

Greene, A.M. and Kirton, G. (2000), 'From Equality to Diversity? The Role of Women-Only Trade Union Education', Paper to *18th International Labour Process Conference*, April, Glasgow.

Greene, A.M., Black, J. and Ackers, P. (2000), 'The Union Makes us Strong? A Study of the Dynamics of Workplace Union Leadership at Two Manufacturing Plants', *British Journal of Industrial Relations*, Vol. 38, 1, pp. 75–95.

Grieco, M. (1987a), 'Family Networks and the Closure of Employment', in G. Lee and R. Loveridge (eds), *The Manufacture of Disadvantage*, Milton Keynes: Oxford University Press.

Grieco, M.S. (1987b), *Keeping it in the Family: Social networks and employment chance*, Tavistock: London.

Grieco, M.S, (1996), *Workers' Dilemmas: Recruitment, reliability and repeated exchange: An analysis of urban social networks and labour circulation*, Routledge: London.

Grieco, M.S, Apt, N. and Turner, G. (1996), *At Christmas and on Rainy Days: transport, travel and the female traders of Accra*, Aldershot: Avebury.

Grijns, M., Smyth, I., Velsen, A.V., Mechfud, S. and Sayago, P. (1994), *Different Women, Different Work: Gender and industrialisation in Indonesia*, Aldershot: Avebury.

Grootaert, C. and Kanbur, R. (1995), 'Child Labour: An economic perspective', *International Labour Review*, Vol. 134, 2, pp. 187–203.

Hakim, C. (1979), 'Occupational Segregation', *Department of Employment Research Paper*, No. 9.

Hakim, C. (1991), 'Grateful Slaves and Self Made Women: Fact and fantasy in women's work orientations', *European Sociological Review*, 7, 2, pp. 101–18.

Hakim, C. (1992), 'Explaining Trends in Occupational Segregation: The measurement, causes and consequences of the sexual division of labour', *European Sociological Review*, Vol. 8, 2, pp. 127–52.

Hakim, C. (1995), 'Five Feminist Myths about Women's Employment', *British Journal of Sociology*, Vol. 46, 3, pp. 429–55.

Hammersley, M. (1992), *What's Wrong with Ethnography?*, London: Macmillan.

Hammersley, M. and Atkinson, P. (1983), *Ethnography, Principles in Practice*, Cambridge University Press.

Hartley, J.F. (1992), 'The Psychology of Industrial Relations', *International Review of Industrial and Organisational Psychology*, Vol. 7, pp. 201–45.

Hartley, J.F. and Stephenson, G.M. (1992), *Employment Relations: The psychology of influence and control at work*, Oxford: Blackwell.

Hartmann, H. (1979), 'Capitalism, Patriarchy and Job Segregation by Sex', in Z. Eisenstein (ed.), *Capitalist Patriarchy and the Case for Socialist Feminism*, New York: Monthly Review Press.

Hawes, W.R. (1999), Book Review of K. Whitfield and G. Strauss (eds) (1998), *British Journal of Industrial Relations*, Vol. 30, 5, pp. 537–9.

Heery, E. and Kelly, J. (1989), 'Full Time Officers and Trade Union Recruitment', *British Journal of Industrial Relations*, Vol. 27, 2, pp. 196–213.

Heery, E., Simms, M., Delbridge, R., Salmon, J. and Simpson, D. (2000), 'The Organising Academy: An assessment', paper presented to the *18th Annual International Labour Process Conference*, April, Glasgow.

Hensman, R. (1988), 'The Gender Division of Labour in Manufacturing Industry: A case study in India', *Institute of Development Studies*, Discussion Paper 253.

Hobsbawm, E.J. and Ranger, T. (eds) (1992), *The Invention of Tradition*, Cambridge University Press.

Hyman, R. (1979), 'The Politics of Work Place Trade Unionism: Recent tendencies and some problems for theory', *Capital and Class*, Vol. 8, pp. 54–67.

Hyman, R. (1999), 'National Industrial Relations Systems and Transnational Challenges: An essay in review', *European Journal of Industrial Relations*, Vol. 5, 1, pp. 89–110.

Hwang, I.K. (1999), 'Globalisation and its Impact on the Korean Labour Sector: A case study of factory workers in Sungnam city', *Korean Social Science Journal*, Vol. 26, 2, pp. 61–93.

Jewson, N. and Mason, D. (1986), 'The Theory and Practice of Equal Opportunities Policies: Liberal and radical approaches', *The Sociological Review*, Vol. 34, 2, pp. 307–34.

Joyce, P. (1980), *Work, Society and Politics: The culture of the factory in later Victorian England*, Oxford: Methuen.

Kapferer, B. (1972), *Strategy and Transaction in an African Factory*, Manchester: Manchester University Press.

Kasturi, L., Brahme, S. and Jhabvala, R. (1990), *Women Workers in India: Studies in employment and status*, Delhi: Chanakya Publications.

Kelly, J. (1994), 'Does the Field of Industrial Relations have a Future?', paper presented to the *British Universities Industrial Relations Asscoiation Conference*, July, Oxford.

Kelly, J. (1996), 'Union Militancy and Social Partnerships', in P. Ackers, C. Smith and P. Smith (eds), *The New Work Place and Trade Unionism*, London: Routledge, pp. 77–109.

Kelly, J. (1998), *Rethinking Industrial Relations: Mobilisation, collectivism and long waves*, London: Routledge.

Kelly, J. and Heery, E. (1994), *Working for the Union*, Cambridge University Press.

Kerfoot, D. and Knights, D. (1994), 'The Gendered Terrain of Paternalism', in S. Wright (ed.), *Anthropology of Organisations*, London: Routledge.

Kirton, G. and Greene, A.M. (2000a), *Managing Diversity: A critical text*, Oxford: Butterworth-Heinemann.

Kirton, G. and Greene, A.M. (2000b), 'Positive Action in Trade Unions: The case of women and Black members', paper presented at the *16th EGOS (European Group of Organisation Studies), Colloquium*, June, Helsinki.

Kirton, G. and Healy, G. (1999), 'Transforming Union Women: The role of women trade union officials in union renewal', *Industrial Relations Journal*, Vol. 30, 1, pp. 31–45.

Kramsjo, B. and Wood, G. (1992), *Breaking the Chains: Collective action for social justice among the rural poor of Bangladesh*, Bangladesh: University Press Ltd.

Kulshereshtha, J.C. (1996), *Child Labour in the Indian Lock Industry*, New Delhi: Uppal Publishing.

Kumari, R. (1998), *Gender Work and Power relations: A case study of Haryan*, New Delhi Har: Anand Publications.

Labour Research (1998), *Hard Work ahead for Unions*, Labour Research Department.

Lawrence, E. (1996), 'Gender and office holding in trade unions', in L. Morris and E.S. Lyon (eds), *Gender Relations in Private and Public*, London: Macmillan.

Lee, E. (1997), *The Labour Movement and the Internet: The new internationalism*, London: Pluto Press.

Legge, K. (1989), 'Human Resource Management: A critical analysis', in J. Storey (ed.), *New Perspectives on HRM*, London: Routledge, pp. 19–40.

Legge, K. (1995), *Human Resource Management: Rhetoric and reality*, London: Macmillan.

Liff, S. (1996), 'Two Routes to Managing Diversity: Individual differences or social group characteristics', *Employee Relations*, Vol. 19, 1, pp. 11–26.

Liff, S. and Wajcman, J. (1996), '"Sameness" and "Difference" Revisited: Which way forward for equal opportunity initiatives?', *Journal of Management Studies*, Vol. 33, 1, pp. 79–95.

Linstead, S. (1993), 'From Post-modern Anthropology to Deconstructive Ethnography', *Human Relations*, Vol. 46, 1, pp. 97–119.

Lockwood, D. (1966), 'Sources of Variation in Working Class Images of Society', *Sociological Review*, Vol. 14, 2, pp. 249–67.

Lown, J. (1983), 'Not So Much a Factory, More a Form of Patriarchy: Gender and class during industrialisation', in E, Gamarnikov (ed.), *Gender, Class and Work*, London: Heinemann, pp. 28–45.

Macdonald, D. (1997), 'Industrial Relations and Globalization: Challenges for employers and their organisations', paper presented at the *International Labour*

Organisation Workshop on Employers' Organisations in Asia-Pacific in the Twenty First Century, Turin, Italy, 5–13 May.

Manwaring, T. (1984), 'The Extended Internal Labour Market', *Cambridge Journal of Economics*, 18, 2, pp. 161–87.

Marchington, M. and Parker, P. (1990), *Changing Patterns of Employee Relations*, Hemel Hempstead: Harvester Wheatsheaf.

Marcus, G. and Cushman, D. (1987), 'Ethnographies as Texts', *Annual Review of Anthropology*, Vol. 11, pp. 215–69.

Marginson, P. (1998), 'The Survey Tradition in British Industrial Relations Research: An assessment of the contribution of large-scale workplace and enterprise surveys', *British Journal of Industrial Relations*, Vol. 36, 3, pp. 361–88.

Margold, J. (1999), 'Reforming the Compliant Image: Filipina activists in the global factory', *Urban Anthropology and Studies of Cultural Systems and World Economic Development*, 28, 1, pp. 1–37.

Marsden, D. (1994), 'Indigenous Management and the Management of Indigenous Knowledge', in S. Wright (ed.), *Anthropology of Organisations*, London: Routledge, pp. 41–56.

Marsh, D. (1992), *The New Politics of British Trade Unionism: Trade union power and the Thatcher legacy*, London: Macmillan.

Martin, R. and Fryer, R. (1975), 'The Deferential Worker?', in M. Bulmer (ed.), *Working Class Images of Society*, London: Routledge.

McCarthy, W. (1994), 'Of Hats and Cattle, or, the Limits of Macro-survey Research in Industrial Relations', *Industrial Relations Journal*, Vol. 25, 4, pp. 315–22.

McIlroy, J. (1998), *Trade Unions in Britain Today*, Manchester University Press.

McInnes, J. (1987), *Thatcherism At Work*, Milton Keynes: Open University Press.

Mies, M. (1988), chapter 2 in T.V. Bennholdt and C. Von Welhof (eds), *Women: The last colony*, London: Zed Books.

Millward, N., Stevens, M., Smart, D. and Hawes, W.R. (1992), *British Work Place Industrial Relations in Transition*, Aldershot: Gower.

Millward, N., Woodland, S., Bryson, A. and Forth, J. (1998), *The British Workplace Industrial Relations Survey Series: A bibliography of research based on WIRS*, London: Policy Studies Institute.

Mohanty, C.J. (1984), 'Under Western Eyes: Feminist scholarship and colonial discourse', *Boundary 2*, Spring/Fall, XII, 3.

Monks, J. (1996), 'The TUC's Stake in Mr. Blair', *The Times*, 17 January.

Morgan, G. and Smircich, L. (1980), 'The Case for Qualitative Research', *Academy of Management Review*, Vol. 5, 4, pp. 491–500.

Morris, T. and Wood, S. (1992), 'Testing the Survey Method: Continuity and change in British industrial relations', *Work, Employment and Society*, Vol. 5, pp. 259–82.

Moulik, T.K. and Purushotham, P. (1986), *Technology Transfer in Rural Industries*, Bombay: Popular Prakashan.

Mukherjee, P.K. (1959), *Economic Surveys in Under-developed Countries: A study in methodology*, London: Asia Publishing House.

OECD (1988), 'Women's Activity Employment and Earnings: A review of recent developments', *OECD Employment Outlook* (Paris), September, pp. 129–72.

Phillips, A. and Taylor, B. (1986), *Sex and Skill in Waged Work: A reader*, Feminist Review, London: Virago.

Pliskin, N., Romm, C.T. and Markey, R. (1997), 'E-mail as a Weapon in an Industrial Dispute', *New technology, Work and Employment*, Vol. 12, 1, pp. 3–12.

Pollert, A. (1981), *Girls, Wives, Factory Lives*, London: Macmillan.

Potter, J. (1996), *Representing Reality: Discourse, Rhetoric and Social Construction*, London: Sage Publications.

Potter, J. and Wetherell, M. (1987), *Discourse and Social Psychology: Beyond Attitudes and Behaviour*, London: Sage Publications.

Prasad, P. and Prasad, A. (2000), 'Casting the Native Subject: Ethnographic practice and the (re)production of difference', paper presented at the *16th EGOS (European Group of Organisation Studies), Colloquium*, June, Helsinki.

Putnam, R.D. (1993), *Making Social Democracy Work: Civic traditions in modern Italy*, Princeton: New Jersey.

Putnam, R.D. (1995), 'Bowling Alone: America's declining social capital', *Journal of Democracy*, Vol. 6, pp. 65–78.

Putnam, R.D. (1998), Plenary Address, 'The Distribution of Social Capital in Contemporary America', *Michigan State University International Conference on Social Capital*, 20–22 April.

Rae, J. (ed.) (1969), *Henry Ford*, Englewood Cliffs: Prentice Hall.

Ramaswamy, E.A. (1977), *The Worker and his Union: A study in South India*, Bombay: Allied Publishers Private Ltd.

Ramaswamy, E.A. (1994), *The Rayon Spinners: The strategic management of industrial relations*, Delhi: Oxford University Press.

Redding, S.G. (1994), 'Comparative Management Theory: Jungle, zoo or fossil bed?', *Organisation Studies*, Vol. 15, 3, pp. 323–59.

Roberts, E. (1996), *A Woman's Place: An oral history or working class women 1840–1940*, Oxford: Blackwell.

Rodgers, G. and Standing, G. (1981), *Child Work, Poverty and Underdevelopment*, Geneva: International Labour Organisation.

Rollinson, D. (1991), 'Attitudes of Trade Union Activists: Some evidence on the Theory of Workplace Incorporation', *Work, Employment and Society*, Vol. 5, 1, pp. 81–100,

Rosaldo, R. (1989), *Culture and Truth: The remaking of social analysis*, Boston: Beacon Press.

Rose, K. (1992), *Where Women are Leaders: The SEWA movement in India*, London: Zed Books.

Roy, D. (1960), 'Banana Time: Job satisfaction and informal interaction', *Human Organisation*, Vol. 18, pp. 156–68.

Rubery, J. and Fagan, C. (1995), 'Comparative Industrial Relations Research: Towards reversing the gender bias', *British Journal of Industrial Relations*, Vol. 33, 2, pp. 209–37.

Saito, H., Wongphanich, M., Karnasouta, S., Kogi, K., Yoshiomi, T. and Kazuhio, S. (1982), *A Comparative Study of Women Workers in the textile industries of Japan and Thailand: A socio-economic profile*, Tokyo: Japan Foundation.

Sathyamurthy, T.V. (1999), 'South Asia: Fifty years after independence', *Soundings*, 11, Spring, pp. 42–66.

Sayce, S. (forthcoming), 'Gender, Family and Community in Black Country Manufacturing', PhD thesis, University of Wolverhampton.

Sayigh, Y. (1958), 'Management–Labour Relations in Selected Arab Countries: Major aspects and determinants', *International Labour Review*, Vol. 77, pp. 519–37.

Scheibl, F. (1996), 'Part Time Workers: Grateful slaves or rational time maximising individuals? An examination of fact and fiction in recent explanations of women's preferences for part time working', *Employment Studies Unit Paper*, 4, University of Hertfordshire.

Sennett, R. (1998), *The Corrosion of Character: The personal consequences of work in the new capitalism*, London and New York: W.W. Norton and Company.

Shostak, A.B. (1999), *Cyberunion: Empowering labor through computer technology*, New York: M.E. Sharpe.

Siegel, B. (1955), 'The Brazilian Cotton Textile Industry 1850–1950', in S. Kutznets, W. Moore and J. Spengler (eds), *Economic growth: Brazil, India, Japan*, Durham: Duke University Press.

Sisson, K. (ed.) (1994), *Personnel Management, a Comprehensive Guide to Theory and Practice in Britain*, Oxford: Blackwell.

Slim, H. and Thompson, P. (1993), *Listening for a Change: Oral testimony and development*, London: Panos.

Srinivas, M.N., Shah, A.M. and Ramaswamy, E.A. (eds) (1979), *The Fieldworker and the Field: Problems and challenge in sociological investigation*, Delhi: Oxford University Press.

Stenner, B. (1989), *The Lockmakers: A century of trade unionism in the lock and safe trade 1889–1989*, Oxford: Malthouse Press.

Terry, M. (1983), 'Shop Steward Development and Managerial Strategies', in G.S. Bain (ed.), *Industrial Relations in Britain*, Oxford: Blackwell.

Terry, M. (1986), 'How Do we Know if Shop Stewards are Getting Weaker?', *British Journal of Industrial Relations*, Vol. 24, pp. 169–80.

Terry, M. (1989), 'Recontextualising Shopfloor Industrial Relations: Some case study evidence', in S. Tailby and C. Whitson (eds), *Manufacturing Change: Industrial relations and reconstructuring*, Oxford: Blackwell, pp. 192–216.

Terry, M. (1995), 'Trade Unions: Shop stewards and the workplace' in P.K. Edwards (ed.), *Industrial Relations: Theory and Practice*, Oxford: Blackwell, pp. 203–28.

Terry, M. and Edwards, P.K. (eds) (1988), *Shopfloor Politics and Controls*, Oxford: Blackwell.

Thompson, E.P. (1993), *Customs in Common*, Harmondsworth: Penguin.

Thompson, P. and Ackroyd, S. (1999), *Organisational Misbehaviour*, London: Sage Publications.

Tilly, C. (1978), *From Mobilization to Revolution*, New York: McGraw Hill.

Treimann, D. and Hartmann, H. (1981), *Women, Work and Wages: Equal pay for work of equal value*, Washington: National Academic Press.

Trench, B. and O'Donnell, S. (1997), 'The Internet and Democratic Participation: Uses of ICTs by voluntary and community organisations in Ireland', *Economic and Social Review*, Vol. 28, 3, pp. 213–34.

Vreeland, H. (1957), *Iran*, New Haven: Human Relations Area Files.

Wacjman, J. (2000), 'Feminism facing industrial relations in Britain', *British Journal of Industrial Relations*, Vol. 38: 2, pp. 183–201.

Waddington, J. and Whitson, C. (1992), ' Why Sign Up? New Trade Union Members Reasons for Joining', *Industrial Relations Review and Report*, 6.

Walton, R.E. and McKersie, R.B. (1965), *A Behavioural Theory of Labor Negotiations: An analysis of a social interaction system*, London and New York: McGraw-Hill.

Warde, A. (1992), 'Industrial Discipline: Factory regime and politics in Lancaster', in A. Sturdy, D. Knights and H. Wilmott (eds), *Skill and Consent: Contemporary studies in the labour process*, London: Routledge.

Watts, M. and Rich, J. (1993), 'Occupational Sex Segregation in Britain 1979–1989: The Persistence of Sexual Stereotyping', *Cambridge Journal of Economics*, Vol. 17, pp. 159–77.

Webb, J. (1997), 'The Politics of Equal Opportunity', *Gender, Work and Organisation*, Vol. 4, 3, pp. 159–69.

Westwood, S. (1984), *All Day, Every Day: Factory and family in the making of women's lives*, London: Pluto.

White, S.C. (1992), *Arguing with the Crocodile: Gender and class in Bangladesh*, Essex: Zed Books.

Whitfield, K. and Strauss, G. (eds) (1999), *Researching the World of Work: Strategies and methods in studying industrial relations*, Cornell University Press.

Wilkinson, B. (1994), 'The Korea Labour "Problem"', *British Journal of Industrial Relations*, Vol. 32, 3, pp. 339–57.

Willis, P. (1977), *Learning to Labour: How working class kids get working class jobs*, Aldershot: Gower.

Wolf, D. (1992), *Factory Daughters: Gender household dynamics and rural industrialisation in Java*, University of California Press.

Wray, D. (1996), 'Paternalism and its Discontents: A case study', *Work, Employment and Society*, Vol. 10, 4, pp. 701–15.

Wright, S. (1994), *Anthropology of Organisations*, London: Routledge.

www.labournet.org.uk

Zeleza, T. (1988), *Labour, Unionisation and Women's Participation in Kenya*, Nairobi: Fredrich-Ubert Foundation.

Index

For Product Safety Concerns and Information please contact our EU
representative GPSR@taylorandfrancis.com
Taylor & Francis Verlag GmbH, Kaufingerstraße 24, 80331 München, Germany

www.ingramcontent.com/pod-product-compliance
Ingram Content Group UK Ltd.
Pitfield, Milton Keynes, MK11 3LW, UK
UKHW022123190926
475702UK00013B/1606

* 9 7 8 0 3 6 7 2 4 9 5 5 7 *